SpringerBriefs in Computer Science

T0171962

SpringerBriefs present concise summaries of cutting-edge research and practical applications across a wide spectrum of fields. Featuring compact volumes of 50 to 125 pages, the series covers a range of content from professional to academic.

Typical topics might include:

- A timely report of state-of-the art analytical techniques
- A bridge between new research results, as published in journal articles, and a contextual literature review
- A snapshot of a hot or emerging topic
- An in-depth case study or clinical example
- A presentation of core concepts that students must understand in order to make independent contributions

Briefs allow authors to present their ideas and readers to absorb them with minimal time investment. Briefs will be published as part of Springer's eBook collection, with millions of users worldwide. In addition, Briefs will be available for individual print and electronic purchase. Briefs are characterized by fast, global electronic dissemination, standard publishing contracts, easy-to-use manuscript preparation and formatting guidelines, and expedited production schedules. We aim for publication 8–12 weeks after acceptance. Both solicited and unsolicited manuscripts are considered for publication in this series.

More information about this series at http://www.springer.com/series/10028

Wolfram Wingerath • Norbert Ritter • Felix Gessert

Real-Time & Stream Data Management

Push-Based Data in Research & Practice

 Springer

Wolfram Wingerath
Baqend GmbH
Hamburg
Hamburg, Germany

Norbert Ritter
University of Hamburg
Hamburg
Hamburg, Germany

Felix Gessert
Baqend GmbH
Hamburg
Hamburg, Germany

ISSN 2191-5768   ISSN 2191-5776   (electronic)
SpringerBriefs in Computer Science
ISBN 978-3-030-10554-9   ISBN 978-3-030-10555-6   (eBook)
https://doi.org/10.1007/978-3-030-10555-6

Library of Congress Control Number: 2018966147

This Springer imprint is published by the registered company Springer Nature Switzerland AG.
The registered company address is: Gewerbestrasse 11, 6330 Cham, Switzerland

Preface

Nowadays, data management systems are facing a multitude of functional application requirements such as query or transaction support. At the same time, nonfunctional requirements like low latency and scalability gain more and more importance, especially in domains where large or even continuously growing volumes of data are to be processed.

Since the beginning of the twenty-first century, it has become obvious that the mature relational database technology fails to meet the ever-increasing, especially nonfunctional requirements. As a consequence, novel (NoSQL) systems sprung up like mushrooms, mainly driven by large internet companies and their need to tackle Big Data management problems. Since each of these systems is geared toward a very specific purpose, though, their respective strengths are usually accompanied by a set of weaknesses—we all have to accept that certain trade-offs need to be managed in order to overcome web-scale data management issues. One of the more notorious examples is the well-known availability-consistency trade-off: Providing a certain guarantee sometimes demands relaxing others!

Facing this new data management system landscape, our Databases and Information Systems research group at the University of Hamburg started a research branch about 10 years ago with the aim to unravel this confusing set of systems. First, we thoroughly analyzed the different systems, classified them according to their specific features and design rationales, and developed a decision guide that helps application developers select the concrete system that meets their application requirements best. Second, we designed a Backend-as-a-Service approach to automatize this selection process and thus unburden system architects from making complex trade-offs during system design. Third, we created a polyglot data management system that seamlessly integrates different NoSQL backend systems with low-latency web caching and scalable stream processing technology in a web-based cloud environment.

The latter was particularly ambitious, since it required extending our view from mostly pull-based NoSQL database systems to other mainly push-based system classes like modern stream processing and real-time database systems. Real-time database systems provide push-based access to database collections, i.e., applications may subscribe to queries in order to receive the result first and then get informed each time the query result changes due to modifications of the underlying database objects. On closer inspection of the currently available real-time database systems, we quickly found that query expressiveness and scalability are often limited by the capabilities of either the subsystem for storage or the subsystem for processing. Thus, system architects and application developers are again forced to deal with difficult trade-offs in order to build real-time applications at scale.

As a consequence, we conducted research explicitly aiming at the design and development of a scalable system for real-time data management. This book not only contains the results of our research but more importantly gives a description of the history of data management from pull-based relational database systems to push-based, scalable real-time data management systems. Since we cannot provide a comprehensive discussion of all available systems in the context of this book, we aim for a good overview over the current state of the art and the different options you have in data management today: This book identifies four elementary data management system classes and characterizes representatives of these classes in detail.

Among the real-time database systems we present in this book is a spin-off of our research group, the Backend-as-a-Service platform Baqend. While we are pretty proud of it, we did our best to paint a neutral picture and provide an objective discussion—see for yourself how the different competitors compare! We are convinced that real-time data processing and push-based result delivery will gain relevance in the near future. May this book be beneficial for everybody who is interested in that area. It is directed toward both practitioners and researchers alike.

Cool to have you on board, have fun while reading!

Hamburg, Germany   Wolfram Wingerath
August 2018   Norbert Ritter
                                                                                Felix Gessert

Contents

About the Authors

Wolfram Wingerath is a distributed systems engineer at the Backend-as-a-Service company Baqend[1] where he is responsible for all things related to real-time query processing. During his PhD studies at the University of Hamburg, Wolfram conceived the scalable design behind Baqend's real-time query engine and thereby also developed a strong background in real-time databases and related technology such as scalable stream processing, NoSQL database systems, cloud computing, and Big Data analytics. Eager to connect with others and share his experiences, Wolfram regularly speaks at developer and research conferences.

Norbert Ritter is a full professor of computer science at the University of Hamburg, where he heads the Databases and Information Systems group. He received his PhD from the University of Kaiserslautern in 1997. His research interests include distributed and federated database systems, transaction processing, caching, cloud data management, information integration, and autonomous database systems. He has been teaching NoSQL topics in various courses for several years. Seeing the many open challenges for NoSQL systems, he and Felix Gessert have been organizing the annual Scalable Cloud Data Management Workshop[2] to promote research in this area.

Felix Gessert is the CEO and co-founder of Baqend[1]. During his PhD studies at the University of Hamburg, he developed the core technology behind Baqend's web performance service. Felix is passionate about making the web faster by bringing research to practice. He frequently talks at conferences about exciting technology trends in data management and web performance.

---

[1] Baqend: https://www.baqend.com/.
[2] Scalable Cloud Data Management Workshop: www.scdm.cloud.

Chapter 1
An Introduction to Real-Time Data Management

In recent years, users have come to expect reactivity from their applications, i.e. they assume that changes made by other users are immediately reflected in the interfaces they are using. Examples are shared worksheets and websites targeting social interaction. These applications require the underlying data storage to publish new and updated information as soon as it is created: Data access is *push-based*. In contrast, traditional **database management** [HSH07] has been tailored towards *pull-based* data access where information is only made available as a direct response to a client request. While triggers and other push-oriented mechanisms have been added to their initial design, they are outperformed by several orders of magnitude when held against natively push-based systems [SC05]. In consequence, the inadequacy of traditional database technology for handling rapidly changing data has been widely accepted as one of the fundamental challenges in database design [SCZ05]. To warrant low-latency updates in quickly evolving domains, systems for **data stream management and processing** [GZ10, Win+16] break with the idea of maintaining a persistent data repository. Instead of random access queries on static collections, they perform sequential, long-running queries or processing tasks over data streams. Data stream management and processing systems thus generate new output whenever new data becomes available and are therefore natively push-based. However, data is only available for processing in one single pass, because data streams are conceptually *unbounded* sequences of data items, infeasible to retain indefinitely.

Database and data stream management, respectively, follow fundamentally different semantics regarding the way that data is processed and accessed as Table 1.1 summarizes. The concept of persistent collections conforms to applications that require a (consistent) view of their domain, for instance to keep track of warehouse stock or do financial accounting. The stream data model, on the other hand, comes natural for domains that facilitate a notion of event sequences or demand reasoning about the relationship between events, for example to analyze stock prices or identify malicious user behavior. However, the access paradigm—pull-based or

© The Author(s), under exclusive license to Springer Nature Switzerland AG 2019
W. Wingerath et al., *Real-Time & Stream Data Management*, SpringerBriefs in
Computer Science, https://doi.org/10.1007/978-3-030-10555-6_1

Table 1.1 A side-by-side comparison of core characteristics of database and data stream management systems

	Database management	Data stream management
Data access	Pull-based	Push-based
Data model	Persistent collection	Ephemeral stream
Query execution	Ad hoc, random access	Continuous, sequential

push-based—is tied to the data model: Database management systems lack support for continuous queries over collections, whereas data stream management systems only provide limited options for persistent data handling.

Acknowledging the gap between database and data stream management systems, a new class of information systems has emerged in recent years that combines collection-based semantics with a push-based access model. These systems are often referred to as **real-time databases**[1] [Puf16, Yu15], because they keep data at the client in-sync with current database state "in realtime" [Pau15], i.e. as soon as possible after change. Popular examples are Firebase, Meteor, and Baqend as discussed in Sect. 3. Like traditional databases, they store consistent snapshots of domain knowledge. But like stream management systems, they allow clients to subscribe to long-running queries that push incremental updates.

In this book, we aim to provide an overview over today's data management systems and their respective aptness for serving data in realtime. To this end, we survey the system space between purely pull-based database management systems on the one side and purely push-based stream management and processing systems on the other.

1.1   A Brief History of Data Management

Unsynchronized access to file systems, network databases (CODASYL), and hierarchical databases (IMS) [FS76] represented the state-of-the-art mechanisms for data storage and retrieval before the advent of relational database systems. However, data management has come a long way since then: Fig. 1.1 provides a coarse-grained overview over the development of data management systems from 1970 until today.

After the introduction of the relational model in 1970 [Cod70], Ingres [Sto+76] and System R [Cha+81] followed shortly thereafter as the first implementations of relational database systems. In the following years, the formalization of data modeling (e.g. through the Entity-Relationship Model [Che75]) and standardization through both ANSI [ANS86] and ISO [Tec87] helped to increase the popularity of relational systems further. While triggers as the first active mechanisms were pro-

---

[1]In this book, we use the terms "real-time database" and "real-time database system" synonymously.

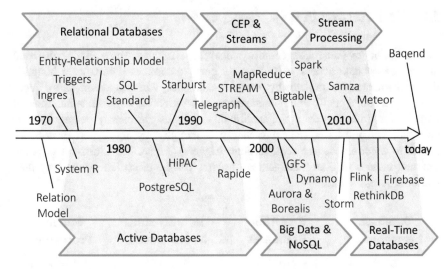

Fig. 1.1   Over the last five decades, different classes of data management systems have been in the focal point of research interest

posed in 1975 already [EC75], active databases such as Starburst [Sch+86], HiPAC [Day+88], and Postgres [SR86] did not emerge before the mid-1980s. Systems like Rapide [San93], Telegraph [Cha+03], STREAM [Mot+03], and Aurora/Borealis [Çet+16] in the 1990s and early 2000s eventually took the acknowledgment of data in motion one step further by introducing dedicated concepts for data streams and event sequences, thus deviating from the relational model centered around static data collections. The explosion of customer data at companies like Google and Amazon in the early 2000s finally sparked development of several data management system classes that parted with the relational model altogether [Ges+16]. NoSQL data stores like BigTable [Cha+06] and Dynamo [DeC+07] revolutionized the way that distributed data stores were designed, favoring high scalability and fault-tolerance over query expressiveness and compliance with existing standards. Similarly, the Google File System (GFS) [GGL03] and MapReduce [DG04] pioneered storage and batch-processing of semi-structured and unstructured huge data volumes and thus turned Big Data management and analytics into hot research topics. Around 2010, stream processing frameworks like Storm [Tos+14], Stratosphere (later renamed to Flink) [ABE+14], and Samza [Nog+17] shifted the research focus from maximizing throughput to also achieving low latency for data-intensive applications at scale. With the growing popularity of interactive and collaborative applications in recent times, real-time database systems like Meteor [Met18], Firebase [Fir16], and Baqend [Baq18] finally received some attention as well as, because they effectively combine the collection-based semantics of traditional databases with the push-based delivery mechanisms known from stream-based systems.

1.2 Data Access: Pull vs. Push

The design of any data management system reflects a bias towards either pull-based or push-based data access: A *pull-based* query assembles data from a bounded data repository and completes by returning data once, whereas a *push-based* query processes a conceptually unbounded stream of information to generate incremental output over time. For example, traditional databases are clearly geared towards efficiency for pull-based data retrieval, even though they do support push-based access to a certain degree (e.g. through triggers). Figure 1.2 illustrates how the different classes of data management systems can be classified by the way they facilitate access to data.

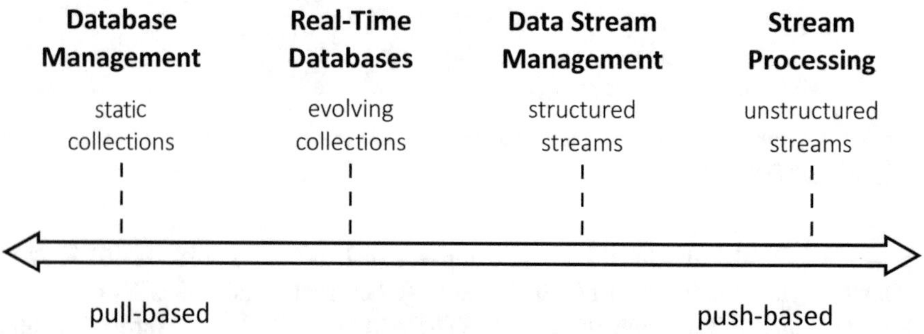

Database Management	**Real-Time Databases**	**Data Stream Management**	**Stream Processing**
static collections	evolving collections	structured streams	unstructured streams

pull-based   push-based

Fig. 1.2 Different classes of data management systems and the access patterns they support

At the one extreme, there are **traditional databases**[2] which represent snapshots of domain knowledge that are the basis of all queries. At the other extreme, there are general-purpose **stream processing** engines which are designed to generate output from conceptually unbounded and arbitrarily structured ephemeral data streams. Real-time databases and data stream management systems both stand in the middle, but adhere to different semantics: **Real-time databases** work on evolving collections that are distinguished from their static counterparts (i.e. from typical database collections) through continuous integration of updates over time, enabling push-based real-time queries. **Data stream management** systems provide APIs to query data streams, for example, by applying filters to incoming data or by computing rolling aggregations and joins over configurable time windows.

---

[2]While we focus on relational database systems in this book, a preference for pull-based over push-based access is also evident in graph databases [Jun+17], object databases [Wie15, Ch. 9], and other databases with non-relational data models [OM10, Ch. 5, Sec. I].

1.3   Query Semantics: Collections vs. Streams

While a database collection represents the current *state* of the application domain, a data stream rather encapsulates recent *change*. For an illustration of the difference between the semantics of collections and streams, consider the example data given in Table 1.2 that shows two different representations of an application for user account management. The **stream**-based representation (a) provides a sequential view on all user actions, but does not retain them indefinitely: Events are available for a certain time window (framed records), but are discarded eventually (lightly shaded records). This view on the data promotes use cases that require notifications, e.g. for individual users logging in or out. However, the system only operates on a suffix and not the entirety of event history. Therefore, queries do not reflect actions that happened long ago: For example, it is not possible to produce a list of all registered users sorted by name or by date of first login, because relevant data is beyond the query's time horizon. In order to serve historical data, the ephemeral events have to be applied to a persistent representation of application state. A database **collection** (b) reflects all data ever written and thus enables queries such as the above-mentioned one. Since collection-based ad hoc queries do not capture events that arrive after the query, though, traditional databases do not propagate informational updates to the client.

Table 1.2 Streams and collections promote different perspectives on data

(a) A data stream primarily captures changes in application state

Timestamp	Name	Action
2017-05-05 07h49	Jane	login
2017-05-05 08h52	Jane	logout
2017-05-06 08h08	Jill	login
2017-05-06 09h32	Ken	login
2017-05-06 09h47	Jill	logout
2017-05-06 10h11	Bob	login
⋮	⋮	⋮

(b) A database collection provides access to the current state of the application

Name	First login	Last login	Logged in
Bob	2017-01-15	2017-05-06	True
Erk	2017-01-26	2017-01-26	False
Jane	2017-02-12	2017-05-05	False
Jill	2016-08-02	2017-05-06	True
Joy	2017-03-09	2017-04-24	False
Ken	2017-05-05	2017-05-06	False
Lee	2016-03-01	2016-04-17	False
Tim	2017-02-23	2017-05-05	False

User account management is just one example of an application domain that requires some form of permanent data storage to answer queries regarding the current state of the world. Given a database's limitation to mainly pull-based access, though, real-time user interfaces are hard to build: One possibility is to reevaluate a given collection-based query from time to time which is inefficient and introduces staleness in the order of the refresh interval (cf. poll-and-diff in Sect. 3.3.1). Another approach is to merge results from collection-based and stream-based queries; thus, the application is effectively burdened with the task of view maintenance which is complex an error-prone (cf. Sect. 2.3).

1.4   Chapter Outline

In the following chapters, we will examine the mechanisms for push-based data access available in the different data management system classes, starting with traditional relational database systems in Chap. 2. Then, we will dissect the most prominent real-time database systems in Chap. 3. In Chap. 4, we will then focus on data stream management systems which do not promote collection-based semantics, but instead view data as potentially infinite streams of information. Subsequently in Chap. 5, we will survey general-purpose stream processing technology and analyze different systems with respect to their capabilities. In our final Chap. 6, we will summarize the big picture, discuss current trends, and project future developments.

References

[ABE+14] Alexander Alexandrov, Rico Bergmann, Stephan Ewen, et al. "The Stratosphere Platform for Big Data Analytics". In: *The VLDB Journal* (2014). ISSN: 1066-8888. doi:10.1007/s00778-014-0357-y URL: http://dx.doi.org/10.1007/s00778-014-0357-y.

[Baq18] Baqend. *Baqend* Accessed: 2018-05-10. 2018. URL: https://www.baqend.com/.

[Cha+03] Sirish Chandrasekaran et al. "TelegraphCQ: Continuous Dataflow Processing". In: *Proceedings of the 2003 ACM SIGMOD International Conference on Management of Data.* SIGMOD '03. San Diego, California: ACM, 2003, pp. 668–668. ISBN: 1-58113-634-X. doi:10.1145/872757.872857. URL: http://doi.acm.org/10.1145/872757.872857.

[Cha+06] Fay Chang et al. "Bigtable: A Distributed Storage System for Structured Data". In: *Proceedings of the 7th USENIX Symposium on Operating Systems Design and Implementation - Volume 7.* OSDI '06. Seattle, WA: USENIX Association, 2006, pp. 15–15. URL: http://dl.acm.org/citation.cfm?id=1267308.1267323.

[Cha+81] Donald D. Chamberlin et al. "A History and Evaluation of System R". In: *Commun. ACM* 24.10 (Oct. 1981), pp. 632–646. ISSN: 0001-0782. doi:10.1145/358769.358784. URL: http://doi.acm.org/10.1145/358769.358784.

[Che75] Peter Pin-Shan Chen. "The Entity-relationship Model: Toward a Unified View of Data". In: *SIGIR Forum* 10.3 (Dec. 1975), pp. 9–9. ISSN: 0163-5840. doi:10.1145/1095277.1095279. **URL:** http://doi.acm.org/10.1145/1095277.1095279.

[Cod70] E. F. Codd. "A Relational Model of Data for Large Shared Data Banks". In: *Commun. ACM* 13.6 (June 1970), pp. 377–387. ISSN: 0001-0782. doi:10.1145/362384.362685. URL: http://doi.acm.org/10.1145/362384.362685.

[Day+88] U. Dayal et al. "The HiPAC Project: Combining Active Databases and Timing Constraints". In: *SIGMOD Rec.* 17.1 (Mar. 1988), pp. 51–70. ISSN: 0163-5808. doi:10.1145/44203.44208. URL: http://doi.acm.org/10.1145/44203.44208.

[DeC+07] G. DeCandia et al. "Dynamo: Amazon's highly available key-value store". In: *ACM SOSP.* Vol. 14. 17. 2007, pp. 205–220. (Visited on 09/12/2012).

[DG04] Jeffrey Dean and Sanjay Ghemawat. "MapReduce: Simplified Data Processing on Large Clusters". In: *Proceedings of the 6th Conference on Symposium on Opearting Systems Design & Implementation - Volume 6.* OSDI'04. San Francisco, CA: USENIX Association, 2004, pp. 10–10. URL: http://dl.acm.org/citation.cfm?id=1251254.1251264.

[EC75] Kapali P. Eswaran and Donald D. Chamberlin. "Functional Specifications of a Subsystem for Data Base Integrity". In: *Proceedings of the 1st International Conference on*

Very Large Data Bases. VLDB '75. Framingham, Massachusetts: ACM, 1975, pp. 48–68. ISBN: 978-1-4503-3920-9. doi:10.1145/1282480.1282484. URL: http://doi.acm.org/10.1145/1282480.1282484.

[Fir16]   Firebase. *Firebase*. Accessed: 2016-09-18. 2016. URL: https://firebase.google.com/.

[FS76]   James P. Fry and Edgar H. Sibley. "Evolution of Data-Base Management Systems". In: *ACM Comput. Surv.* 8.1 (Mar. 1976), pp. 7–42. ISSN: 0360-0300. doi:10.1145/356662.356664. URL: http://doi.acm.org/10.1145/356662.356664.

[Ges+16]   Felix Gessert et al. "NoSQL Database Systems: A Survey and Decision Guidance". In: *Computer Science - Research and Development* (2016).

[GGL03]   Sanjay Ghemawat, Howard Gobioff, and Shun-Tak Leung. "The Google File System". In: *Proceedings of the Nineteenth ACM Symposium on Operating Systems Principles*. SOSP '03. Bolton Landing, NY, USA: ACM, 2003, pp. 29–43. ISBN: 1-58113-757-5. doi:10.1145/945445.945450. URL: http://doi.acm.org/10.1145/945445.945450.

[GZ10]   Lukasz Golab and M. Tamer Zsu. *Data Stream Management*. Morgan & Claypool Publishers, 2010. ISBN: 1608452727, 9781608452729.

[HSH07]   Joseph M. Hellerstein, Michael Stonebraker, and James Hamilton. "Architecture of a Database System". In: *Found. Trends databases* 1.2 (Feb. 2007), pp. 141–259. ISSN: 1931-7883. doi:10.1561/1900000002. URL: http://dx.doi.org/10.1561/1900000002.

[Jun+17]   Martin Junghanns et al. "Handbook of Big Data Technologies". In: ed. by Albert Y. Zomaya and Sherif Sakr. Springer International Publishing, 2017. Chap. Management and Analysis of Big Graph Data: Current Systems and Open Challenges, pp. 457–505. ISBN: 978-3-319-49340-4. doi:10.1007/978-3-319-49340-4_14. URL: https://doi.org/10.1007/978-3-319-49340-4_14.

[Mot+03]   Rajeev Motwani et al. "Query Processing, Approximation, and Resource Management in a Data Stream Management System". In: *CIDR* 2003.

[Nog+17]   Shadi A. Noghabi et al. "Samza: Stateful Scalable Stream Processing at LinkedIn". In: *Proc. VLDB Endow.* 10.12 (Aug. 2017), pp. 1634–1645. ISSN: 2150-8097. doi:10.14778/3137765.3137770. URL: https://doi.org/10.14778/3137765.3137770.

[OM10]   James A. O'Brien and George M. Marakas. *Management Information Systems*. 10th Edition. McGraw-Hill/Irwin, 2010.

[Pau15]   Ryan Paul. "Build a realtime liveblog with RethinkDB and PubNub". In: *RethinkDB Blog* (May 2015). Accessed: 2017-05-20. URL: https://rethinkdb.com/blog/rethinkdb-pubnub/.

[Puf16]   Frank van Puffelen. "Have you met the Realtime Database?" In: *Fire-base Blog* (July 2016). Accessed: 2017-05-20. URL: https://firebase.googleblog.com/2016/07/have-you-met-realtime-database.html.

[San93]   Alexandre Santoro. *Case Study in Prototyping With Rapide: Shared Memory Multiprocessor System*. Tech. rep. Stanford University, Mar. 1993.

[SC05]   Michael Stonebraker and Ugur Cetintemel. " "One Size Fits All": An Idea Whose Time Has Come and Gone". In: *Proceedings of the 21st International Conference on Data Engineering*. ICDE '05. Washington, DC, USA: IEEE Computer Society, 2005, pp. 2–11. ISBN: 0-7695-2285-8. doi:10.1109/ICDE.2005.1. URL: http://dx.doi.org/10.1109/ICDE.2005.1.

[Sch+86]   P. Schwarz et al. "Extensibility in the Starburst Database System". In: *Proceedings on the 1986 International Workshop on Object-oriented Database Systems*. OODS '86. Pacific Grove, California, USA: IEEE Computer Society Press, 1986, pp. 85–92. ISBN: 0-8186-0734-3. URL: http://dl.acm.org/citation.cfm?id=318826.318842.

[SCZ05]   Michael Stonebraker Uğur Cetintemel, and Stan Zdonik. "The 8 Requirements of Real-time Stream Processing". In: *SIGMOD Rec.* 34.4 (Dec. 2005), pp. 42–47. ISSN: 0163-5808. doi:10.1145/1107499.1107504. URL: http://doi.acm.org/10.1145/1107499.1107504.

[SR86]   Michael Stonebraker and Lawrence A. Rowe. "The Design of POSTGRES". In: *Proceedings of the 1986 ACM SIGMOD International Conference on Management of Data*. SIGMOD '86. Washington, D.C., USA: ACM, 1986, pp. 340–355. ISBN: 0-89791-191-1. doi:10.1145/16894.16888. URL: http://doi.acm.org/10.1145/16894.16888.

[Sto+76]   Michael Stonebraker et al. "The Design and Implementation of INGRES". In: *ACM Trans. Database Syst.* 1.3 (Sept. 1976), pp. 189–222. ISSN: 0362-5915. doi:10.1145/320473.320476. URL: http://doi.acm.org/10.1145/320473.320476.

[Tos+14]   Ankit Toshniwal et al. "Storm@Twitter". In: *Proceedings of the 2014 ACM SIGMOD International Conference on Management of Data.* SIGMOD '14. Snowbird, Utah, USA: ACM, 2014, pp. 147–156. ISBN: 978-1-4503-2376-5. doi:10.1145/2588555.2595641. URL: http://doi.acm.org/10.1145/2588555.2595641.

[Wie15]   Lena Wiese. *Advanced Data Management for SQL, NoSQL, Cloud and Distributed Databases.* DeGruyter 2015. ISBN: 978-3-11-044140-6. URL: http://wiese.free.fr/adm.html.

[Win+16]   Wolfram Wingerath et al. "Real-time stream processing for Big Data". In: *it - Information Technology* 58.4 (2016), pp. 186–194. doi:10.1515/itit-2016-0002. URL: http://dx.doi.org/10.1515/itit-2016-0002.

[Yu15]   Alice Yu. "What does it mean to be a real-time database? — Slava Kim at Devshop SF May 2015". In: *Meteor Blog* (June 2015). Accessed: 2017-05-20.

[ANS86]   ANSI. *X3.135-1986: Information Systems – Database Language – SQL.* Standard. American National Standards Institute, Oct. 1986.

[Met18]   Meteor Development Group. *Meteor.* Accessed: 2018-05-10. 2018.URL: https://www.meteor.com/.

[Tec87]   Technical Committee: ISO/IEC JTC 1 Information Technology. *ISO 9075:1987: Information processing systems – Database language – SQL.* Standard. International Organization for Standardization, June 1987.

[Çet+16]   Uğur Çetintemel et al. "The Aurora and Borealis Stream Processing Engines". In: *Data Stream Management: Processing High-Speed Data Streams.* Ed. by Minos Garofalakis, Johannes Gehrke, and Rajeev Rastogi. Berlin, Heidelberg: Springer Berlin Heidelberg, 2016, pp. 337–359. ISBN: 978-3-540-28608-0.

Chapter 2
Database Management

The first databases were **hierarchical and network databases** [TL76], developed during the 1960s. They exposed procedural query interfaces (as opposed to descriptive ones), so that accessing specific information in one of these systems was similar to navigating to a specific file within a file system [FS76]. Early query languages were severely limited in expressiveness and relied on high-level programming languages for scanning and search [Cod71, Sec. 1.2]. Similarly, consistency checks were mostly enforced within client applications and evolved around conventions and best practices [Oll06]. In consequence, data integrity was difficult to maintain and reorganizing or scaling a database could be disruptive for existing client applications. During the 1970s, standards in database management (especially regarding query languages) [FS76] and data independence received more attention within the database community [Cod71, Sec. 2]. The proposition of the **relational model** [Cod70] then eventually led to a descriptive query language that evolved into the *Structured Query Language (SQL)* [CB74].

2.1 Triggers and Active Databases

Relational databases were initially designed as *passive* repositories that accept, modify, or retrieve structured data as a direct response to an explicit request [Cod82]. Acknowledging the need to model application behavior in addition to the structural aspects of a domain, database **triggers** were the first *active* mechanisms to be proposed for relational database systems [EC75] that became part of the SQL standard [CPM96]. Essentially, triggers are procedures that are implicitly invoked on database events such as insert, update, or delete operations or on system events like errors or user logins [Ora, Sec. 3.2]. As such, they are primarily used as a means to enforce integrity or to propagate writes on specific entities to depending entities [Sto86]. In an effort to facilitate more sophisticated behavioral semantics,

© The Author(s), under exclusive license to Springer Nature Switzerland AG 2019
W. Wingerath et al., *Real-Time & Stream Data Management*, SpringerBriefs in
Computer Science, https://doi.org/10.1007/978-3-030-10555-6_2

event-condition-action (ECA) rules [SKM92] were introduced to database systems during the 1980s and 1990s. ECA rules capture more complex *events* (cf. Sect. 4.4), for example with temporal components (e.g. a fixed date or a time period) or compositions (e.g. disjunctions or sequences of specific occurrences) [Cha95]. Further, execution of an action is not only tied to the occurrence of a specified event, but typically also depends on fulfillment of a corresponding *condition*, for example a predicate over database state or the triggering event's net effect (i.e. the difference between state before and after the event) [HW93, Sec. 4.1].

The usefulness of **active databases** [Mor83, PD99], i.e. database systems with advanced active features, is often illustrated with applications like materialized view maintenance [Sto+90] and real-time user interface (UI) updates [Dʃ94]. However, common to all centralized active database implementations is that database-internal active mechanisms quickly become performance bottlenecks [SD95]. Therefore, some approaches restrict semantics to avoid infeasible scenarios; for example, Alert [Sch+91] supports active rules exclusively over append-only tables. Comparable sacrifices are made by **real-time (active) databases** [Pur+93, Ram+96].[1] In order to deliver predictable execution times, real-time (active) databases relax consistency guarantees, reduce concurrency, or restrict query and rule expressiveness [Eri98]. To this day, active database mechanisms remain prohibitive for scalability and thus even modern database systems are documented to display poor latency and throughput when active features are used at scale (see for example [Bli+16, p. 13]). Implementing active facilities *on top of* an existing database system (as opposed to implementing them as an internal component) is usually even less efficient [GGD95] [SKM92, Sec. 4.1] and significantly more difficult, as the information required for detecting events is often only available within the database [PD99, Sec. 7.1].

2.2   Change Data Capture, Cache Coherence, and Time-Series Data

Given the limitations of active mechanisms within database systems, more generic approaches have been sought to make informational updates available outside of the database system. Systems for **change data capture (CDC)** [Kle16, Ch. 11] extract data from the primary storage system and propagate it to other systems, e.g. for replication purposes, invalidation of cached views, or for custom data processing pipelines. Some systems use *trigger-based replication*, i.e. they employ active

---

[1]The underlying notion of the term "real-time" in this context refers to compliance with time constraints, whereas real-time database systems discussed in Chap. 3 are "real-time" in the sense that they detect and propagate updated information with low latency. For details, we refer to the term disambiguation in Sect. 3.1.

mechanisms to persist updates to auxiliary tables which, in turn, are then polled periodically by downstream systems. For instance, Databus extracts data through this pattern from Oracle databases [Das+12, Sec. 4.1] and Bucardo [Mul14, Mul11] extracts data from PostgreSQL through triggers and notification listeners (cf. page 13). However, the auxiliary tables dedicated to storing change information can become write bottlenecks and using triggers for data replication is rather error-prone in itself because of the complexity involved in replicating multiple tables or ensuring transactional visibility of updates [Das+12]. To avoid these difficulties, some systems attach to the database using lower-level database protocols: As one example, Databus hooks into MySQL's storage engine API to obtain a change log [Das+12, Sec. 4.2]. There are also various products accompanying commercial databases that implement inter-database replication using proprietary protocols (e.g. Oracle's Active Data Guard [Datb]) or provide database change logs for external applications (e.g. Oracle's GoldenGate [Gol] or IBM's InfoSphere CDC [Inf]). Even though some systems provide simple mechanisms to filter extracted data by a user-defined predicate (e.g. Databus [Das+12, Sec. 4.3]), more complex transformations or processing is usually performed in dedicated (stream processing) systems such as the ones discussed in Chaps. 4 and 5.

Change data capture can be used to feed **distributed caches** or **memory grids** which offload read and write workload from the main database system or perform processing tasks such as data transformation. For example, systems like Oracle Cache Coherence [Bli+16], Hazelcast [Luc+17], or Ignite [Ign] are deployed as server clusters which act as write-through or write-behind caches between client applications and the primary data storage. The cached entities are stored in a derived format (e.g. Java objects) and relate to the application data model rather than the underlying database schema. Use of filter queries is discouraged, because they are processed node-locally and thus require heavyweight scatter-gather patterns for result assembly (see for example Hazelcast [Luc+17, Sec. 5.14] or Oracle Cache Coherence [Bli+16, p. 5]). Even though these systems provide limited support for SQL or SQL-like query languages, data is usually accessed by primary key and in a programmatic fashion, i.e. through program code. Under the term **continuous queries** [Haz] [Ruz+11, Ch. 23] [Wit+07], some systems offer push-based filter queries with stream-based semantics or even collection-based static filter predicates and result ordering (e.g. Oracle Cache Coherence [Ruz+14a, Ruz+14b]), similar to the functionality provided by the real-time database systems discussed in Chap. 3.

Timeseries databases [DF14] (e.g. OpenTSDB [Sig+18] or DalmatinerDB [Pro18]) are specialized in storing and querying conceptually infinite sequences of events as a function of their time of occurrence, for example sensor data indexed by time. While some of them (e.g. InfluxDB [Inf16]) are capable of rolling averages or other continuous aggregations [BD91], they are typically employed for analytic queries, or downsampling streams of information; their capabilities do not extend to change notifications as provided by real-time database systems.

2.3   Materialized Views

Since results of complex queries cannot be maintained up-to-date efficiently by the database-external systems discussed above, sophisticated mechanisms for database-internal query result caching have been developed. The idea behind **materialized views** [BC79, CY12] is to precompute the result of particularly expensive queries, so that they do not have to be evaluated repeatedly, but can be served immediately when requested. **Logical views**, in contrast, are rewritten to queries that have to be evaluated on every request. Thus, materialized views are significantly faster to access than logical views. However, this read time performance advantage comes at a hefty cost: In order to guarantee freshness of the cached query result, changes[2] have to be detected and applied at write time.

View maintenance algorithms can be classified according to whether they assume full or only partial access to the underlying database tables [GM99]. **Recomputation** of a query result is conceptually straightforward, applicable to arbitrarily complex queries, and obviously requires unrestricted access to the base data. While queries with relatively stable results can theoretically be maintained fresh and consistent by just recomputing the result after every invalidating write operation, it is difficult to distinguish invalidating writes from those that can be safely ignored: A host of literature is dedicated to recognizing updates that change the query result (*relevant updates*) [BLT86, BCL89, Elk90, LS93], so that recomputation can be avoided unless required for consistency. In order to address queries that evolve more quickly or for which the base data is not accessible, **incremental view maintenance** [Vis96] avoids recomputation altogether by detecting and applying changes directly to the materialized result. Even though incremental maintenance of query results has been studied for other data models as well (e.g. object databases [Nak01]), the majority of literature refers to relational databases [CY12, GM99]. To decouple the maintenance process from access to the base data, **self-maintainability** [GJSM96] has received particular attention in the context of materialized views: It postulates that a view can be kept up-to-date using only the view contents and the incoming modifications (i.e. the database writes). In practice, many queries are not self-maintainable per se, but only with respect to specific modifications at runtime or with the help of auxiliary data [Qua+96]. For example, sorted queries are not inherently self-maintainable with respect to deletes and updates, because removing one item from the result may cause an unrelated item to enter the result from beyond limit; it is possible, however, to make a top-k query self-maintainable with respect to *a certain number* of updates or deletes by initially requesting a top-k' result where $k > k'$ [Yi+03]. Thus, there is often a trade-off between

---

[2]In the context of view maintenance in relational (SQL) databases, it is not only important to update a materialized view whenever records in the corresponding base tables are written, but also when the view definition is altered or when one of the base table's schema is modified. We do not go into detail here in order to keep the focus on result maintenance and refer to [CY12, Sec. 2.5.1] and [NLR98] for more information.

the usefulness of additional auxiliary data during maintenance and the costs of initially assembling it. Taking the middle ground between recomputation and incremental maintenance, some algorithms only materialize and incrementally maintain auxiliary data (e.g. a subquery result or a join index) instead of the actual result [BM90]. This kind of **partial maintenance** of a materialized view still necessitates reevaluating the query to refresh, but makes this process very cheap. At the same time, the maintained auxiliary data can be used by the database optimizer to accelerate other queries as well [Vis98]. A materialized view can thus be understood as a data structure that speeds up database reads, similar to a *database index*. Since both recomputation and incremental maintenance of a query result can be very resource-intensive, maintaining very complex or a great number of materialized views is sometimes performed under relaxed consistency guarantees to allow distributing or deferring the maintenance process [Agr+09]: When stale data is tolerable, incremental maintenance can be performed through asynchronous and throughput-optimized batch updates [Sal+00]; likewise, recomputation can be deferred to save resources. When tables are spread or sharded across different physical nodes, materialized views are typically maintained in deferred fashion, because the overhead for transferring data between different sites is significant and sometimes prohibitive for immediate change propagation [Lab+00]. Maintenance of **materialized views in distributed environments** has been researched for decades, specifically in the context of data warehousing where queries tend to be particularly expensive to compute [Cha+09, BKS00, SP89]. Instead of maintaining individual queries or indices, entire database partitions are sometimes mirrored to remote sites in these scenarios, so that queries can be executed locally (i.e. at the replica) that would otherwise have to be executed remotely (i.e. at the primary). In these distributed setups, the transitions between indexing, materialized view maintenance, and database replication can therefore be fluent.

2.4   Change Notifications

Using mechanisms related to change detection in materialized views [Notb], some relational database systems have the ability to send notifications when previously requested data has changed or might have changed. Most implementations exhibit occasional false positives, i.e. change notifications may be sent without an actual data change occurring [Nota, Note, MK+17]. In contrast to **continuous query subscriptions** in stream management systems or real-time databases, change notification messages in relational database systems *do not carry the changed data itself*, but only identifiers (e.g. row IDs, table names or query identifiers) and some information on what happened (e.g. the type of operation or a text message). Therefore, supposedly changed data items or queries have to be requested again after a notification has been received in order to make sure the local copy is still up-to-date [Nota, Notd][MK+17, Sec. 15.5].

Like materialized views, change notifications serve the overall purpose of improving ad hoc query performance in domains *where updates are infrequent* [Notc][MK+17, Sec. 15.5]. As typical use cases, vendors describe three-tier applications where data is cached in the middle tier and *only few queries* have to be monitored for changes [MK+17, Sec. 15.7.7]. When receiving user requests, the middle-tier application servers respond on the basis of their local copies of the data which they refresh asynchronously when receiving a notification [Notf] [MK+17, Sec. 15.5]. To receive change notifications, application servers can subscribe to specific data items or queries, thus launching a process at the database that monitors ongoing operations and detects relevant changes. Since monitoring a query for changes incurs additional work on write operations, more than a few concurrently active registered queries may impair online transaction processing (OLTP) throughput [Notc][MK+17, Sec. 15.7.7]. For scenarios with high throughput or many unique queries, some vendors explicitly discourage using their notification feature and instead recommend employing workarounds, for example using triggers or implementing sophisticated middleware for change detection [Notc].

2.5 Summary and Discussion

Traditional databases offer limited capabilities to push information to clients. Triggers, ECA rules, and change notifications cannot be used for proactive data delivery, unless brittle workarounds are employed. A few systems provide continuous that do provide push-based data access, but these systems are typically limited in both expressiveness and scalability. While materialized views employ mechanisms that are suitable for providing real-time queries, they are exclusively used to increase pull-based query performance and do not provide push-based access to data.

References

[Agr+09] Parag Agrawal et al. "Asynchronous View Maintenance for VLSD Databases". In: *Proceedings of the 2009 ACM SIGMOD International Conference on Management of Data*. SIGMOD '09. Providence, Rhode Island, USA: ACM, 2009, pp. 179–192. ISBN: 978-1-60558-551-2. DOI: 10.1145/1559845.1559866. URL: http://doi.acm.org/10.1145/1559845.1559866.

[BC79] O. Peter Buneman and Eric K. Clemons. "Efficiently Monitoring Relational Databases". In: *ACM Trans. Database Syst.* 4.3 (Sept. 1979), pp. 368–382. ISSN: 0362-5915. DOI: 10.1145/320083.320099. URL: http://doi.acm.org/10.1145/320083.320099.

[BCL89] José A. Blakeley, Neil Coburn, and Per-Ake Larson. "Updating Derived Relations: Detecting Irrelevant and Autonomously Computable Updates". In: *ACM Trans. Database Syst.* 14.3 (Sept. 1989), pp. 369–400. ISSN: 0362-5915. DOI: 10.1145/68012.68015. URL: http://doi.acm.org/10.1145/68012.68015.

[BD91]   Peter J. Brockwell and Richard A. Davis. *Time Series: Theory and Methods*. 2nd Edition. Springer Science & Business Media, 1991.

[BKS00] Ladjel Bellatreche, Kamalakar Karlapalem, and Michel Schneider. "On Efficient Storage Space Distribution Among Materialized Views and Indices in Data Warehousing Environments". In: *Proceedings of the Ninth International Conference on Information and Knowledge Management*. CIKM '00. McLean, Virginia, USA: ACM, 2000, pp. 397–404. ISBN: 1-58113-320-0. DOI: 10.1145/354756.354846. URL: http://doi.acm.org/10.1145/354756.354846.

[Bli+16] Craig Blitz et al. *Oracle Coherence 12c: Planning a Successful Deployment*. Tech. rep. Oracle Corporation, June 2016.

[BLT86] José A. Blakeley, Per-Ake Larson, and Frank Wm Tompa. "Efficiently Updating Materialized Views". In: *SIGMOD Rec.* 15.2 (June 1986), pp. 61–71. ISSN: 0163-5808. DOI: 10.1145/16856.16861. URL: http://doi.acm.org/10.1145/16856.16861.

[BM90]   José A. Blakeley and Nancy L. Martin. "Join Index, Materialized View, and Hybrid-Hash Join: A Performance Analysis". In: *Proceedings of the Sixth International Conference on Data Engineering*. Washington, DC, USA: IEEE Computer Society, 1990, pp. 256–263. ISBN: 0-8186-2025-0. URL: http://dl.acm.org/citation.cfm?id=645475.654167.

[CB74]   Donald D. Chamberlin and Raymond F. Boyce. "SEQUEL: A Structured English Query Language". In: *Proceedings of the 1974 ACM SIGFIDET (Now SIGMOD) Workshop on Data Description, Access and Control*. SIGFIDET '74. Ann Arbor, Michigan: ACM, 1974, pp. 249–264. DOI: 10.1145/800296.811515. URL: http://doi.acm.org/10.1145/800296.811515.

[Cha+09] Leonardo Weiss F. Chaves et al. "Towards Materialized View Selection for Distributed Databases". In: *Proceedings of the 12th International Conference on Extending Database Technology: Advances in Database Technology*. EDBT '09. Saint Petersburg, Russia: ACM, 2009, pp. 1088–1099. ISBN: 978-1-60558-422-5. DOI: 10.1145/1516360.1516484. URL: http://doi.acm.org/10.1145/1516360.1516484.

[Cha95] Sharma Chakravarthy. "Early Active Database Efforts: A Capsule Summary". In: *IEEE Trans. on Knowl. and Data Eng.* 7.6 (Dec. 1995), pp. 1008–1010. ISSN: 1041-4347. DOI: 10.1109/69.476505. URL: http://dx.doi.org/10.1109/69.476505.

[Cod70] E. F. Codd. "A Relational Model of Data for Large Shared Data Banks". In: *Commun. ACM* 13.6 (June 1970), pp. 377–387. ISSN: 0001-0782. DOI: 10.1145/362384.362685. URL: http://doi.acm.org/10.1145/362384.362685.

[Cod71] E. F. Codd. "A Data Base Sublanguage Founded on the Relational Calculus". In: *Proceedings of the 1971 ACM SIGFIDET (Now SIGMOD) Workshop on Data Description, Access and Control*. SIGFIDET '71. San Diego, California: ACM, 1971, pp. 35–68. DOI: 10.1145/1734714.1734718. URL: http://doi.acm.org/10.1145/1734714.1734718.

[Cod82] E. F. Codd. "Relational Database: A Practical Foundation for Productivity". In: *Commun. ACM* 25.2 (Feb. 1982), pp. 109–117. ISSN: 0001-0782. DOI: 10.1145/358396.358400. URL: http://doi.acm.org/10.1145/358396.358400.

[CPM96] Roberta Cochrane, Hamid Pirahesh, and Nelson Mendonça Mattos. "Integrating Triggers and Declarative Constraints in SQL Database Systems". In: *Proceedings of the 22th International Conference on Very Large Data Bases*. VLDB '96. San Francisco, CA, USA: Morgan Kaufmann Publishers Inc., 1996, pp. 567–578. ISBN: 1-55860-382-4. URL: http://dl.acm.org/citation.cfm?id=645922.673498.

[CY12]   Rada Chirkova and Jun Yang. "Materialized Views". In: *Foundations and Trends in Databases* 4.4 (2012), pp. 295–405. ISSN: 1931-7883. DOI: 10.1561/1900000020. URL: http://dx.doi.org/10.1561/1900000020.

[D+94]   Oscar Díaz et al. "Supporting Dynamic Displays Using Active Rules". In: *SIGMOD Rec.* 23.1 (Mar. 1994), pp. 21–26. ISSN: 0163-5808. DOI: 10.1145/181550.181555. URL: http://doi.acm.org/10.1145/181550.181555.

[Das+12] Shirshanka Das et al. "All Aboard the Databus!: Linkedin's Scalable Consistent
          Change Data Capture Platform". In: *Proceedings of the Third ACM Symposium
          on Cloud Computing*. SoCC '12. San Jose, California: ACM, 2012, 18:1–18:14.
          ISBN: 978-1-4503-1761-0. DOI: 10.1145/2391229.2391247. URL: http://doi.
          acm.org/10.1145/2391229.2391247.

  [Datb] *Oracle Active Data Guard: Real-Time Data Protection and Availability*. Oracle. Oct.
          2015.

  [DF14] Ted Dunning and Ellen Friedman. *Time Series Databases: New Ways to Store and
          Access Data*. Ed. by Mike Loukides. O'Reilly Media, Nov. 2014.

  [EC75] Kapali P. Eswaran and Donald D. Chamberlin. "Functional Specifications of a Sub-
          system for Data Base Integrity". In: *Proceedings of the 1st International Conference
          on Very Large Data Bases*. VLDB '75. Framingham, Massachusetts: ACM, 1975,
          pp. 48–68. ISBN: 978-1-4503-3920-9. DOI: 10.1145/1282480.1282484. URL:
          http://doi.acm.org/10.1145/1282480.1282484.

  [Elk90] Charles Elkan. "Independence of Logic Database Queries and Update". In: *Pro-
          ceedings of the Ninth ACM SIGACT-SIGMOD-SIGART Symposium on Principles of
          Database Systems*. PODS '90. Nashville, Tennessee, USA: ACM, 1990, pp. 154–160.
          ISBN: 0-89791-352-3. DOI: 10.1145/298514.298557. URL: http://doi.acm.org/
          10.1145/298514.298557.

  [Eri98] Joakim Eriksson. "Real-Time and Active Databases: A Survey". In: *Active, Real-Time,
          and Temporal Database Systems: Second International Workshop, ARTDB-97 Como,
          Italy, September 8–9, 1997 Proceedings*. Ed. by Sten F. Andler and Jörgen Hansson.
          Berlin, Heidelberg: Springer Berlin Heidelberg, 1998, pp. 1–23. ISBN: 978-3-540-
          49151-4. DOI: 10.1007/3-540-49151-1_1. URL: http://dx.doi.org/10.1007/3-
          540-49151-1_1.

  [FS76] James P. Fry and Edgar H. Sibley. "Evolution of Data-Base Management Sys-
          tems". In: *ACM Comput. Surv.* 8.1 (Mar. 1976), pp. 7–42. ISSN: 0360-0300. DOI:
          10.1145/356662.356664. URL: http://doi.acm.org/10.1145/356662.356664.

 [GGD95] Andreas Geppert, Stella Gatziu, and Klaus R. Dittrich. "A designer's benchmark for
          active database management systems: 007 meets the BEAST". In: *Rules in Database
          Systems: Second International Workshop, RIDS '95 Glyfada, Athens, Greece Septem-
          ber 25–27, 1995 Proceedings*. Ed. by Timos Sellis. Berlin, Heidelberg: Springer
          Berlin Heidelberg, 1995, pp. 309–323. ISBN: 978-3-540-45137-2.

[GJSM96] Ashish Gupta, H. V. Jagadish, and Inderpal Singh Mumick. "Data integration using
          self-maintainable views". In: *Advances in Database Technology – EDBT '96: 5th
          International Conference on Extending Database Technology Avignon, France, March
          25–29, 1996 Proceedings*. Ed. by Peter Apers, Mokrane Bouzeghoub, and Georges
          Gardarin. Berlin, Heidelberg: Springer Berlin Heidelberg, 1996, pp. 140–144. ISBN:
          978-3-540-49943-5. DOI: 10.1007/BFb0014149. URL: http://dx.doi.org/10.1007/
          BFb0014149.

  [GM99] Ashish Gupta and Iderpal Singh Mumick. *Materialized views: techniques, implemen-
          tations, and applications*. MIT press, 1999. ISBN: 0-262-57122-6.

   [Gol] *Oracle GoldenGate 12c: Real-Time Access to Real-Time Information*. Oracle. Mar
          2015.

   [Haz] *Hazelcast: Continuous Query Cache*. Accessed: 2017-11-12. Hazelcast. 2017. URL:
          http://docs.hazelcast.org/docs/latest-development/manual/html/Distributed_Query/
          Continuous_Query_Cache.html

 [HW93]   E. Hanson and J. Widom. *An Overview of Production Rules in Database Systems*.
          Technical Report 1993-18. Stanford University, 1993. URL: http://ilpubs.stanford.edu:
          8090/25/.

   [Ign] *Introducing Apache Ignite^{TM}*. GridGain Systems Inc. 2017.

[Inf] *Overview of InfoSphere CDC (IBM Infosphere Change Data Capture, Version 6.5.2)*. Accessed: 2017-11-12. IBM. 2011. URL: https://www.ibm.com/support/knowledgecenter/en/SSTRGZ_10.1.3/com.ibm.cdcdoc.mcadminguide.doc/concepts/overview_of_cdc.html.

[Kle16] Martin Kleppmann. *Designing Data-Intensive Applications: The Big Ideas Behind Reliable, Scalable, and Maintainable Systems*. O'Reilly, 2016.

[Lab+00] Wilburt Labio et al. "Performance Issues in Incremental Warehouse Maintenance". In: *Proceedings of the 26th International Conference on Very Large Data Bases*. VLDB '00. San Francisco, CA, USA: Morgan Kaufmann Publishers Inc., 2000, pp. 461–472. ISBN: 1-55860-715-3. URL: http://dl.acm.org/citation.cfm?id=645926.671684.

[LS93] Alon Y. Levy and Yehoshua Sagiv. "Queries Independent of Updates". In: *Proceedings of the 19th International Conference on Very Large Data Bases*. VLDB '93. San Francisco, CA, USA: Morgan Kaufmann Publishers Inc., 1993, pp. 171–181. ISBN: 1-55860-152-X. URL: http://dl.acm.org/citation.cfm?id=645919.672674.

[Luc+17] Greg Luck et al. *Mastering Hazelcast IMDG*. Tech. rep. Hazelcast, Feb. 2017.

[MK+17] Chuck Murray, Tom Kyte, et al. "Using Continuous Query Notification (CQN)". In: *Oracle Database Development Guide, 12c Release 1 (12.1)*. Oracle, May 2017.

[Mor83] Matthew Morgenstern. "Active Databases As a Paradigm for Enhanced Computing Environments". In: *Proceedings of the 9th International Conference on Very Large Data Bases VLDB '83*. San Francisco, CA, USA: Morgan Kaufmann Publishers Inc., 1983, pp. 34–42. ISBN: 0-934613-15-X. URL: http://dl.acm.org/citation.cfm?id=645911.671127.

[Mul11] Greg Sabino Mullane. "NOTIFY vs. Prepared Transactions in Postgres(the Bucardo solution)". In: *End Point Blog* (May 2011). Accessed:2017-11-12. URL: https://www.endpoint.com/blog/2011/05/03/notify-vs-prepared-transactions-in.

[Mul14] Greg Sabino Mullane. "Version 5 of Bucardo database replication system". In: *End Point Blog* (June 2014). Accessed: 2017-11-12. URL: https://www.endpoint.com/blog/2014/06/23/bucardo-5-multimaster-postgres-released.

[Nak01] Hiroaki Nakamura. "Incremental Computation of Complex Object Queries". In: *Proceedings of the 16th ACM SIGPLAN Conference on Object- oriented Programming Systems, Languages, and Applications*. OOPSLA '01. Tampa Bay FL, USA: ACM, 2001, pp. 156–165. ISBN: 1-58113-335-9. DOI: 10.1145/504282.504294 URL: http://doi.acm.org/10.1145/504282.504294.

[NLR98] Anisoara Nica, Amy J. Lee, and Elke A. Rundensteiner. "The CVS Algorithm for View Synchronization in Evolvable Large-Scale Information Systems". In: *Proceedings of the 6th International Conference on Extending Database Technology: Advances in Database Technology*. EDBT '98. Berlin, Heidelberg: Springer-Verlag, 1998, pp.359–373. ISBN: 3-540-64264-1. URL: http://dlacmorg/citation.cfm?id=645338.757494.

[Nota] *PostgreSQL 9.6 Documentation: Notify*. Accessed: 2017-05-13. The PostgreSQL Global Development Group. 2017. url: https://www.postgresql.org/docs/9.6/static/sql-notify.html.

[Notb] *SQL Server 2008 R2 Books Online: Creating a Query for Notification*. Accessed: 2017-05-12. Microsoft. 2017. URL:https://msdn.microsoft.com/en-us/library/ms181122.aspx.

[Notc] *SQL Server 2008 R2 Books Online: Planning for Notifications*. Accessed: 2017-05-12. Microsoft. 2017. URL: https://technet.microsoftcom/en-us/library/ms187528(v=sql105).aspx#Anchor_1.

[Notd] *SQL Server 2008 R2 Books Online: Query Notification Messages*. Accessed: 2017-05-13. Microsoft. 2017. URL: https://msdn.microsoft.com/en-us/library/ms189308(v=sql.105).aspx.

[Note] *SQL Server 2008 R2 Books Online: Understanding When Query Notifications Occur*. Accessed: 2017-05-15. Microsoft. 2017. URL: https://msdn.microsoft.com/en-us/library/ms188323(v=sql.105).aspx.

[Notf] *SQL Server 2008 R2 Books Online: Using Query Notifications*. Accessed: 2017-05-13. Microsoft. 2017. URL: https://technet.microsoft.com/en-us/library/ms175110(v=sql105).aspx.

[Oll06] T William Olle. "Nineteen Sixties History of Data Base Management".In: *History of Computing and Education 2 (HCE2): IFIP 19th World Computer Congress, WG 9.7, TC 9: History of Computing Proceedings of the Second Conference on the History of Computing and Education, August 21–24, 2006, Santiago, Chile* Ed. by John Impagliazzo. Boston, MA: Springer US, 2006, pp. 67–75.ISBN: 978-0-387-34741-7. DOI:10.1007/978-0-387-34741-7_4. URL: https://doi.org/10.1007/978-0-387-34741-7_4.

[Ora] *Oracle Database Development Guide 12c Release 1 (12.1)* Oracle.May 2016.

[PD99] Norman W.Paton and Oscar Díaz. "Active Database Systems". In: *ACM Comput. Surv.* 31.1 (Mar. 1999), pp. 63–103. ISSN: 0360-0300. DOI:10.1145/311531.311623. URL: http://doi.acm.org/10.1145/311531.311623.

[Pur+93] B. Purimetla et al. *A Study of Distributed Real-Time Active Database Applications* Tech. rep. Amherst, MA, USA, 1993.

[Qua+96] Dallan Quass et al. "Making Views Self-maintainable for Data Warehousing". In: *Proceedings of the Fourth International Conference on Parallel and Distributed Information Systems*. DIS'96.MiamiBeach,Florida, USA: IEEE Computer Society, 1996, pp. 158–169. ISBN: 0-8186-7475-X. URL: http://dl.acm.org/citation.cfm?id=382006.383205.

[Ram+96] Krithi Ramamritham et al. "Integrating Temporal, Real-time, an Active Databases". In: *SIGMOD Rec.* 25.1 (Mar 1996), pp. 8–12. ISSN: 0163-5808. DOI: 10.1145/381854.381868. URL: http://doi.acm.org/10.1145/381854.381868.

[Ruz+11] Joseph Ruzzi et al. *Oracle Coherence Developer's Guide Release 3.7.1*2011.

[Ruz+14a] Joseph Ruzzi et al. "Querying Data In a Cache". In: *Oracle Fusion Middleware: Developing Applications with Oracle Coherence, 12c (12.1.2)*. Oracle,May 2014.

[Ruz+14b] Joseph Ruzzi et al. "Using Continuous Query Caching". In: *Oracle Fusion Middleware: Developing Applications with Oracle Coherence, 12c (12.1.2)* Oracle, May 2014.

[Sal+00] Kenneth Salem et al. "How to Roll a Join: Asynchronous Incremental View Maintenance". In: *SIGMOD Rec.* 29.2 (May 2000), pp. 129–140. ISSN:0163-5808. DOI: 10.1145/335191.335393. URL: http://doi.acm.org/10.1145/335191.335393.

[Sch+91] Ulf Schreier et al. "Alert: An Architecture for Transforming a Passive DBMS into an Active DBMS". In: *Proceedings of the 17th International Conference on Very Large Data Bases*. VLDB '91. San Francisco, CA, USA:Morgan Kaufmann Publishers Inc., 1991, pp. 469–478. ISBN: 1-55860-150-3. URL: http://dl.acm.org/citation.cfm?id=645917.672314.

[SD95] Eric Simon and Angelika Kotz Dittrich. "Promises and Realities of Active Database Systems". In: *Proceedings of the 21th International Conference on Very Large Data Bases*. VLDB '95. San Francisco, CA, USA: Morgan Kaufmann Publishers Inc., 1995, pp. 642–653. ISBN: 1-55860-379-4. URL: http://dl.acm.org/citationcfm?id=645921.673319.

[Sig+18] Benoît Sigoure et al. *OpenTSDB* Accessed: 2018-05-10. 2018. url: http://opentsdb.net/.

[SKM92] Eric Simon, Jerry Kiernan, and Christophe de Maindreville. "Implementing High Level Active Rules on Top of a Relational DBMS". In: *Proceedings of the 18th International Conference on Very Large Data Bases*. VLDB '92. San Francisco, CA, USA: Morgan Kaufmann Publishers Inc., 1992,pp. 315–326. ISBN: 1-55860-151-1. URL: http://dl.acm.org/citation.cfm?id=645918.672488.

[SP89] Arie Segev and Jooseok Park. "Maintaining Materialized Views in Distributed Databases". In: *Proceedings of the Fifth International Conference on Data Engineering*. Washington, DC, USA: IEEE Computer Society 1989, pp. 262–270. ISBN: 0-8186-1915-5. URL: http://dl.acm.org/citation.cfm?id=645474.653729

[Sto+90] Michael Stonebraker et al. "On Rules, Procedure, Caching and Views in Data Base Systems". In: *Proceedings of the 1990 ACM SIGMOD Inter- national Conference on Management of Data*. SIGMOD '90. Atlantic City New Jersey USA:ACM, 1990, pp. 281–290. ISBN: 0-89791-365-5. DOI: 10.1145/93597.98737. URL:http://doi.acm.org/ 10.1145/93597.98737.

[Sto86] Michael Stonebraker. "Object Management in POSTGRES Using Procedures". In: *Proceedings on the 1986 International Workshop on Object- oriented Database Systems*. OODS '86. Pacific Grove, California, USA: IEEE Computer Society Press, 1986, pp. 66–72. ISBN: 0-8186-0734-3. URL: http://dl.acm.org/citation.cfm? id=318826.318840.

[TL76] D. C. Tsichritzis and F H. Lochovsky. "Hierarchical Data-Base Management: A Survey". In: *ACM Comput. Surv* 8.1 (Mar 1976), pp.105–123. ISSN: 0360-0300. DOI: 10.1145/356662.356667. URL: http://doi.acm.org/10.1145/356662.356667.

[Vis96] Dimitri Vista. "Optimizing incremental view maintenance expressions in relational databases". PhD thesis. University of Toronto, 1996.

[Vis98] Dimitra Vista. "Integration of incremental view maintenance into query optimizers". In: *Advances in Database Technology — EDBT'98: 6th International Conference on Extending Database Technology Valencia, Spain, March 23–27, 1998 Proceedings*. Ed. by Hans-Jörg Schek et al. Berlin,Heidelberg: Springer Berlin Heidelberg, 1998. Chap. EDBT 1998: Advances in Database Technology — EDBT'98, pp. 374–388.textscisbn: 978-3-540-69709-1. DOI: 10.1007/BFb0100997. textscurl: https://doi. org/10.1007/BFb0100997.

[Wit+07] Andrew Witkowski et al. "Continuous Queries in Oracle". In: *Proceedings of the 33rd International Conference on Very Large Data Bases*. VLDB '07. Vienna, Austria: VLDB Endowment, 2007, pp. 1173–1184. ISBN:978-1-59593-649-3. URL: http://dl. acm.org/citation.cfm?id=1325851.1325985.

[Yi+03] Ke Yi et al. "Efficient Maintenance of Materialized Top-k Views". In: *Proceedings of the 19th International Conference on Data Engineering* (2003).

[Inf16] InfluxData Inc. *InfluxDB* Accessed: 2016-09-18.2016. URL: https://www.influxdata. com/time-series-platform/influxdb/.

[Pro18] Project FiFo. *DalmatinerDB* Accessed: 2018-05-10.2018. URL: https://dalmatiner.io/.

Chapter 3
Real-Time Databases

While traditional database systems are targeted at providing a consistent snapshot of the application domain, real-time databases acknowledge that data may evolve. Both the architectures and client APIs of real-time databases reflect that facts can change over time and that the system may have to enhance or correct issued information. Real-time databases may allow snapshot (one-time) queries over database collections or they may provide interfaces to directly access the stream of update operations. But their defining property is that queries are formulated as though they were evaluated on static data collections, even when their response is a continuous stream of updates to the query result.

In this chapter, we scrutinize the current state of the art in real-time databases with respect to how the individual systems provide real-time queries.

3.1 What Is a Real-Time Database?

In the past, the term "real-time databases" has been used as a reference to specialized pull-based databases that produce an output within strict timing constraints [Pur+93, AH98, Eri98]. Within the scope of this book, however, **real-time databases** are systems that provide push-based access to database collections. Likewise, **real-time queries** in the context of this book are push-based queries on top of database *collections*. They follow the same collection-based querying semantics as common database queries, but respond with a continuous stream of informational updates in addition to the initial query result. In the literature, contrastingly, the term "real-time query" sometimes refers to a particular form of ad hoc pull-based query [TS+09] or to a push-based query over data streams [Ros11]; we do not share this notion of real-time queries in this book. Correspondingly, **real-time applications** are reactive or interactive applications that make new information available to the user as soon as possible after they have been committed to storage [Eri98]. This book addresses

W. Wingerath et al., *Real-Time & Stream Data Management*, SpringerBriefs in Computer Science, https://doi.org/10.1007/978-3-030-10555-6_3

applications with soft timing constraints and specifically does not address security-critical or other applications that impose strict upper bounds on response times such as flight control systems or nuclear power plant controls [Sta88].

3.2   What Is a Real-Time Query?

Intuitively, the information delivered by a real-time database through a real-time query has two components: the initial result and change events. Both inherit certain characteristics from data returned by database and data stream management systems, respectively. The **initial result** corresponds to the data returned by a common ad hoc database query and thus captures the data items matching on request. It is assembled from persistent storage, just like a common database query result. **Change events** (also called change notifications) are sent whenever the result is altered (e.g. when a matching data item is inserted). Thus, they capture how the result evolves over time. Through change events, the client receives all information required to maintain the initial result up-to-date.

There are two distinct types of real-time database queries that differ in the way they expose data to the application: **Event stream queries** simply present the raw change events to the application, so that it can maintain an up-to-date copy of the result or apply custom business logic. **Self-maintaining queries** are more abstract as they do the result maintenance in transparent manner and provide the client with the complete (updated) query result on every change (instead of just the change delta). Using the latter, reactive behavior can be implemented without any notion of data streams or change events built into the business logic.

Changes in a query result are gathered through a continuous process that sifts through the database write stream, similar to a continuous query in a stream management system. In order to identify the relevant updates for a given real-time query, the database has to inspect every single write operation that might possibly affect the query result. This task is straightforward for some queries and rather complicated for others. We only address simple filter queries (i.e. select-project queries [Bad09]) in this book and refer to [Win18] for a discussion of more complex real-time queries that involve ordering, joins, or aggregations.

The decision tree in Fig. 3.1 illustrates how this task can be translated to two simple questions asked for any written data item[1]:

1. Does the item match the query now? ("Is match?")
2. Did the item match the query before? ("Was match?")

When a data item matches the query after an insert or update (left branch), it is either an already-matching item that was altered (*change*) or a former non-match that just entered the result (*add*). Similarly, whenever a data item is deleted or does not match

---

[1] While the depicted approach does not apply to set operations, an update that affects several data items can be transformed into a set of single-item updates to make the approach applicable.

the query after an insert or update (right branch), it either is a matching item that just left the result (*remove*) or it does not relate to the query result whatsoever (*none*).

In the presence of many concurrent real-time queries or high update throughput, this continuous monitoring process becomes very expensive. To put the resource requirements into perspective, consider an app with 1000 concurrent users and an average throughput of 1000 written data items per second. Given each user has only one active real-time query to filter a string attribute by some pattern, the real-

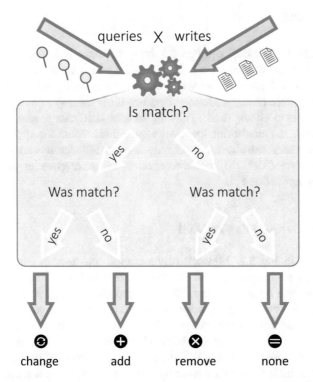

Fig. 3.1 A real-time database has to match all real-time queries (blue arrow) against all incoming write operations (red arrow) to generate change notifications on result alterations (green arrows)

time database already may have to perform one million matching operations—every single second. And this does not account for more complex queries: Sorted queries may require additional work to maintain result order and enforce limit or offset clauses. Similarly, queries with joins or aggregations may impose even higher **overhead**, because they necessitate maintaining counters, intermediate results, or other data structures that are implicitly required to maintain the actual query result. It is possible to apply "optimizations" (e.g. batching) that trade throughput for increased latency. Likewise, complexity may not be quadratic for query expressions that allow efficient indexing (e.g. comparisons). But if minimal latency is mandatory, there is no alternative to considering every write operation in the context of every active real-time query. To warrant feasibility, this has to be implemented in a scalable manner.

3.3 System Landscape

In this section, we discuss the most popular real-time databases available today. Since no standards have been established in this field of data management, we analyze individual system architectures for this purpose.

3.3.1 Meteor

Meteor [Met18] is a JavaScript app development framework that targets reactive apps and websites. It uses MongoDB as its internal data storage and therefore inherits its query expressiveness while adding self-maintaining and event stream queries on top. Interestingly, Meteor offers two different implementations to detect relevant changes to a query result: The original approach (*change monitoring + poll-and-diff*) combines monitoring local write operations within the application server and periodic query reevaluation; it is only used as fallback nowadays. The more recent (and current default) implementation (*oplog tailing*) relies on monitoring MongoDB's replication log.

Change Monitoring + Poll-and-Diff

As illustrated in Fig. 3.2, Meteor's original approach towards real-time queries combines two mechanisms that detect changes received by the server itself (blue) and those received by another server (red), respectively: First, a Meteor application server performs local **change monitoring** to discover state changes that are relevant for currently active real-time queries. Thus, a newly inserted object (1) is not only forwarded to the database (2), but is also translated to a corresponding query change delta for every matching real-time query (3). However, change monitoring alone is not sufficient in multi-server deployments: Server-local monitoring done within the server on the left (A), for example, will not capture write operations received by the server on the right (B). To compensate for this fact, Meteor employs a second strategy called **poll-and-diff** which essentially reevaluates a real-time query periodically ("poll"), computes relative changes to the locally maintained result ("diff"), and then sends them to the client (4). When these two strategies are combined, the client will receive a relevant update either immediately through change monitoring (red) or after a short delay upon discovery through poll-and-diff (blue).

From the client perspective, poll-and-diff has the obvious disadvantage of potential staleness windows bounded by the polling interval (default: 10 s). With unfortunate timing, result updates can also go completely unnoticed; for example, an item entering and leaving the result between query polls will not be registered at all. But even if an application can tolerate multi-second lags and missed notifications, poll-and-diff becomes infeasible when many real-time queries are active concurrently. This is because each one of them induces processing overhead on the database system through periodic polling. In numbers, 1000 query subscriptions result in an average of 100 queries per second whose results have to be (1) assembled and (2) serialized, then (3) be sent to the application server where they are (4) deserialized again, so that they can finally (5) be analyzed for relevant changes. While this may be tractable in some cases, it quickly gets prohibitively expensive when results are large. Further, it should be pointed out that this is just what happens in an otherwise idle system, i.e. when no data is being written whatsoever. The situation gets worse when write throughput increases, because the database has less spare resources to serve periodic poll queries and because each application

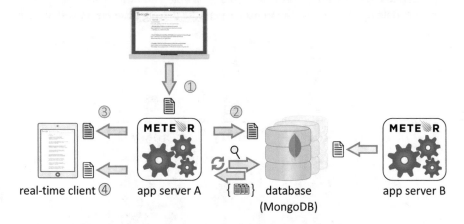

Fig. 3.2 Poll-and-diff: Meteor executes a query again and again to discover changes

server has to spend more CPU time on change monitoring—which becomes more demanding with an increasing number of active real-time queries as well. It should be noted that poll-and-diff works for arbitrary queries, since the pull-based query mechanisms of the underlying database are used. At the same time, though, it is important to understand that real-time queries that rely exclusively on poll-and-diff (i.e. queries that are not supported by change monitoring) implicitly expose latency in the order of the polling interval.

Oplog Tailing

Seeing the considerable downsides of poll-and-diff, the Meteor developers came up with an alternative approach that has a different set of trade-offs. As described above, a Meteor application server is able to maintain a query result by itself, given it receives all relevant write operations. However, since a write operation is only visible to the application server that receives it, multi-server deployments require a mechanism that informs all servers about write operations received by the others. The poll-and-diff approach accomplishes this, but at the same time introduces high base load by executing the same query over and over. Acknowledging this problem, *oplog tailing* was introduced as an alternative solution that uses MongoDB's replication protocol to feed the full write stream to every application server.

MongoDB achieves write scalability by distributing data across different partitions (*shards*). In a production deployment, data within a partition is kept redundantly in a so-called **replica set**: Write operations within a partition are first applied by the *primary* and then delivered to the *secondaries*. Internally, the primary logs all writes in a *capped collection*—a ring buffer called the **oplog**—and the secondaries are following along using *tailable cursors* [Mon]. The basic idea of oplog tailing [Col16] is to have the Meteor application servers hook into MongoDB replication as though they were secondaries. As illustrated in Fig. 3.3, each application server taps into each primary's oplog and thus will never miss a single update operation. This setup makes periodic polling obsolete and eliminates

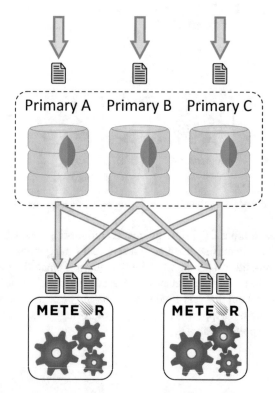

Fig. 3.3 With oplog tailing, each Meteor application server receives all MongoDB writes: Thus, OLTP workload is sharded, but real-time workload is not

the staleness inherent to poll-and-diff. But in doing so, it introduces the application server as a bottleneck for write throughput. Because this is where Meteor deviates from the way that MongoDB uses the oplog: While each MongoDB secondary has to keep up with only one primary, each Meteor server has to keep up with the combined throughput of the *entire MongoDB cluster*. As a consequence, MongoDB can scale with write throughput, but Meteor cannot.

This is not just a theoretical limitation, but a critical problem for production deployments: It is a known issue [Wor+14] that load spikes can saturate and take down a Meteor application server when oplog tailing is enabled [Mao+14]. To address this particular issue, poll-and-diff is used as a fallback strategy [Met15] for oplog tailing whenever an application server falls behind in monitoring the change log. But this is obviously associated with the cost of potential staleness and becomes infeasible as well when there are more than a few active real-time queries [Kat+15]. To leverage maximum performance, it is therefore *officially recommended* to carefully evaluate—on a per-query basis—whether to enable or disable oplog tailing [Met16].

As a sidenote, oplog tailing does not eliminate the need to contact the database completely. For an example, consider a real-time query for the top-3 baccarat players as depicted in Fig. 3.4. The maintaining server receives a partial update to a previously unknown player: According to the received update, Bobby has a higher score than any baccarat player. However, it is unknown whether Bobby is a baccarat

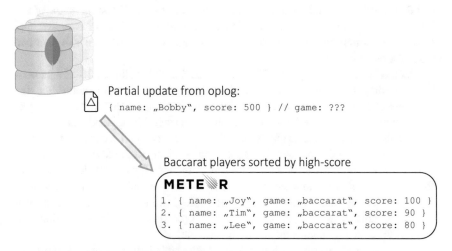

Partial update from oplog:
{ name: „Bobby", score: 500 } // game: ???

Baccarat players sorted by high-score

METE◣R
1. { name: „Joy", game: „baccarat", score: 100 }
2. { name: „Tim", game: „baccarat", score: 90 }
3. { name: „Lee", game: „baccarat", score: 80 }

Fig. 3.4 Information delivered through the oplog can be insufficient to decide whether or not an update has an effect on a given query's result

player to begin with, because the oplog does not tell: It only contains information on Bobby's new score (500), but not the associated game. In consequence, the Meteor application server has to query MongoDB for Bobby's associated game in order to determine whether the query is affected by Bobby's new high score.

In summary, Meteor offers two implementations of real-time queries: Poll-and-diff facilitates expressive real-time queries, but can be laggy and only works when few real-time queries are active. Oplog tailing is viable in the presence of many concurrent real-time queries, but is only feasible for low write throughput, because it effectively circumvents the sharding mechanism of the underlying database. Neither approach works for many users and high throughput.

3.3.2   RethinkDB

RethinkDB [Ret16] is a JSON document store with query expressiveness comparable to MongoDB's. However, RethinkDB is a completely independent project that
seems more ambitious than MongoDB in some areas, offering advanced features
like pull-based θ-join queries [Mar16]. Among the more interesting specialties of
RethinkDB are *changefeeds*: real-time queries with an event stream query interface.

Changefeeds

RethinkDB's technique of change discovery is very similar to Meteor's oplog
tailing: Clients do not communicate with the database nodes directly, but instead
with the application server [Mew16]; each application server runs an instance of
the **RethinkDB proxy**, a process that relays communication between clients and
the RethinkDB cluster. A client registers a real-time query at a RethinkDB proxy
and then receives the initial result and a stream of change deltas: the *changefeed*.
The RethinkDB proxy, in turn, queries the database once on subscription and
subsequently monitors all write operations from the RethinkDB cluster to maintain
the real-time query result.

Just like Meteor with oplog tailing, RethinkDB nullifies all benefits of database-
level sharding by burdening individual application servers with monitoring the
complete cluster write stream. Due to this write bottleneck, RethinkDB is subject
to the same performance limitations as oplog tailing: Changefeeds cannot scale
beyond the capacity of a single application server and will saturate application
server resources under pressure. In contrast to Meteor, RethinkDB does not rely
on external technical artifacts such as the oplog, though. Thus, in particular, internal
change propagation is more elegant and does not require additional round-trips to
fill informational gaps, as is the case with oplog tailing (cf. Fig. 3.4). But even
though RethinkDB executes the concept behind oplog tailing in cleaner fashion than
Meteor, the concept remains inherently unscalable.

There are few reports of RethinkDB users and their experiences with the
scalability of changefeeds. However, CoCalc (formerly known as SageMathCloud)
[CoC18] as one of the most enthusiastic RethinkDB users reverted from RethinkDB
to PostgreSQL for a reactive web application, because a makeshift solution based
on PostgreSQL's change notifications (cf. Sect. 2.4) outperformed RethinkDB
changefeeds by an order of magnitude [Ste17].

In brief, RethinkDB offers a real-time query implementation similar to Meteor's
oplog tailing: Write throughput for RethinkDB's real-time queries does not scale
as it is bottlenecked by single-node capacity. Unlike Meteor, RethinkDB does not
have a poll-and-diff-like approach to utilize the pull-based query API for real-
time queries. Thus, the pull-based interface is more expressive than the push-based
one. For example, changefeeds for sorted queries support a limit, but no offset
[Mar15]. Further, the client API has *no self-maintaining queries*. In order to keep
a query result up-to-date, the application logic therefore has to implement result
maintenance on top of an event stream query.

3.3.3 Parse

Similar to Meteor, Parse is an app development framework that uses MongoDB as its backing store. It was immensely popular and had one of the largest MongoDB deployments world-wide around the year 2015 [Ges17]. While Meteor and RethinkDB have provided real-time queries since 2012 and 2014, respectively, Parse announced the feature in March 2016 [Wan16b]—after they had announced their own shutdown [Lac16]. In this section, we describe the *Live Query* feature that brings event stream queries to the Parse platform.

Live Queries

Without any support for sorting [Wan16a], Parse's real-time queries are less expressive than those of its peers, even though the architecture itself is very similar. Parse's Live Query mechanism bears a strong resemblance to Meteor's oplog tailing and RethinkDB's changefeeds: Each real-time query is maintained by a single process, the **LiveQuery Server**. Likewise, single-server matching performance is the hard limit for write throughput. In contrast to Meteor and RethinkDB, though, Parse entertains separate processes for OLTP workload (application server) and for real-time query matching (LiveQuery server). Further, application servers publish their change log into a Redis-based message queue instead of handing them directly to the matching processors; this increases scalability and further decouples failure of the query matching process from the main application server. While the approach in itself remains unscalable by design, the Parse implementation appears less likely to break in an overload scenario. This statement cannot be validated, though, because we are not aware of any major projects using Parse Live Queries.

To summarize, the Parse LiveQuery architecture bears resemblance to Meteor's oplog tailing and RethinkDB's changefeeds. Thus, real-time queries do not scale with write throughput and query expressiveness is limited in comparison to pull-based queries: Sorted real-time queries are not supported at all. Like RethinkDB, Parse has no *no self-maintaining queries*, but only an event-based real-time query interface.

3.3.4 Firebase

Unlike the other systems discussed in this section, **Firebase** [Fir16] is a proprietary service and only very little is known about the technology stack behind its interfaces. Certain hard limits are known, though, beyond which a single instance will not scale [Fire]; for example, more than 100,000 parallel client connections or more than 1000 write operations per second are not supported [Fira]. Firebase has been developed since 2011 and was acquired by Google in 2014 [Tam14]. Even though the core service is often advertised as a "real-time database" [Puf16], it can arguably be better described as a service for cross-device state synchronization due to a very restrictive query interface. Over the years, additional functionality has been added to the Firebase ecosystem through other services, e.g. for authentication, asset hosting, and performance monitoring [Tam16].

Data Modeling and Querying

In contrast to other JSON-based data stores, the original Firebase data model is not represented by a collection of JSON documents, but by one single JSON document: a cloud-hosted tree structure of nested objects and lists. In order to access data, a client essentially has to navigate through the hierarchy and request specific child nodes for which it will receive immediate updates when data is modified by others. Thus, Firebase is natively push-based. However, Firebase only provides little querying capabilities beyond simple lookups by primary key, so that it can be difficult to map application requirements to the simplistic access model Firebase exhibits. The only way to deviate from access by key is to apply a *single* static filter (no logical AND/OR) or to enforce order on a *single* attribute. Filter expressiveness is limited to lookups ($=$) and range queries ($<, \leq, >, \geq$); in particular, content-based filtering (e.g. through regex queries) is not supported [Ric13, Leh14] and usually implemented by employing third-party services or systems such as Elasticsearch [Ric14]. For use cases that require more sophistication (e.g. ordering by surname and then by forename), the Firebase team recommends employing workarounds like introducing artificial attributes (e.g. the composite of two other attributes) or retrieving a superset of all relevant data and doing the actual query processing in the client [Wen15]. Likewise, nesting data is officially discouraged [Fir17], because it makes fine-grained access control impractical and data retrieval more expensive: Since Firebase only allows fetching data subtrees entirely (i.e. including their child nodes), high-level nodes in a deeply-nested tree structure become more bloated as their child count grows. However, flattening out data structures often takes away even more of the expressiveness, since one-to-one and one-to-many relationships are naturally expressed through nesting in the document data model [SF12].

Advanced Queries with Firestore

In late 2017, Firestore was introduced as a document-oriented real-time database service that aims to provide increased scalability and more advanced querying capabilities compared to the original Firebase [Duf17, Fira]. In contrast to the original real-time database service, data in Firestore is organized in a collection of JSON documents rather than one single huge JSON document; thus, Firestore facilitates data retrieval in a more fine-grained fashion. Another relevant improvement is support for composite queries through filter chaining (logical AND). However, these improvements come with certain restrictions: First, it is only possible to combine range expressions and lookups on the same attribute or to combine lookup expressions on different attributes [Fird]. Put differently, range expressions on different attributes as well as filter disjunction (logical OR) are not supported by either the original Firebase nor Firestore. Regarding sorting, Firestore imposes some restrictions as well: If a query contains a range expression, the first sorting key must be the attribute over which the range expression is evaluated [Firc]. Thus, a query such as "Find all citizens older than 20 and younger than 30 years, sorted by hometown" is still not feasible. Firestore has been built upon work from Google's Cloud Datastore [Goo18, Tam17] and thus inherits some traits and limitations from the underlying systems. Like Megastore [Bak+11], specifically, Firestore provides transactions, but also imposes harsh limits on write throughput: With only 500 writes/s per collection and even only 1 write/s per document [Firb], Firestore bars itself from write-heavy applications, similar to Firebase with its restriction to 1000 writes/s across the entire data set. Firestore further exhibits latency which is several 100 ms higher than Firebase's [Ker17]. Like the original Firebase, Firestore does not support regex queries or comparable content-based filters [Fird].

To conclude, Firebase does not suffer from the scalability bottlenecks apparent in the design of Meteor's, RethinkDB's, or Parse's real-time query implementations, but also does not feature sophisticated query mechanisms. Even though denormalizing the data model or evaluating queries in the client can compensate the lack of query expressiveness to a certain degree, sophisticated query patterns tend to be inefficient and awkward to implement [Jam16, Ros16, Bov17].

3.3.5 Baqend

Baqend [Baq18] is a fully managed web and app development platform similar to Firebase, but is built on top of the pull-based database MongoDB like Meteor, RethinkDB, and Parse. As an important distinction to the other real-time database systems discussed in this book, however, Baqend offloads the expensive task of real-time query matching to a standalone subsystem that is completely isolated from the application server. Baqend's subsystem for real-time queries is called **InvaliDB**[2] [Win18] and it is based on the stream processing framework Storm [Tos+14]. Data exchange between the application server and InvaliDB is implemented through a distributed message queue based on Redis [San18].

---

[2]InvaliDB's name is derived from its usage within the Quaestor architecture [Ges+17] where it invalidates cached database queries. The Quaestor architecture implements a scheme for global caching of dynamic content, specifically database query results. Within the Quaestor architecture, InvaliDB is used to detect modifications to query results, so that stale caches can be invalidated in a timely manner.

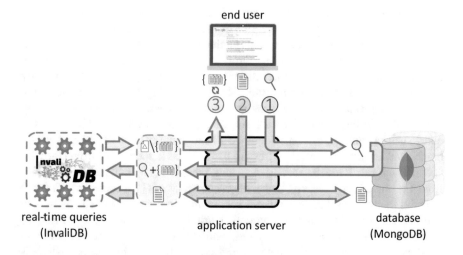

end user

real-time queries
(InvaliDB)

application server

database
(MongoDB)

Fig. 3.5 Baqend strictly separates responsibilities for data storage (MongoDB) from real-time query matching (InvaliDB). For serving real-time queries, the application server only runs the lightweight InvaliDB client which relays messages between the end users, MongoDB, and InvaliDB

Figure 3.5 illustrates how information is routed between an end user, the application server, the database, and InvaliDB in order to enable real-time queries. For subscribing to a real-time query (1), a web or mobile application sends a subscription request to an application server which then forwards this request to InvaliDB. If there already is an active subscription for this query, InvaliDB activates the subscription immediately by sending out an acknowledgment which is forwarded to the subscriber by the application server; if there is no active subscription for the query yet, InvaliDB requests the current result from the application server (which in turn queries the database to retrieve it) before activating the subscription. In order to enable result change detection with low latency, InvaliDB needs to be fed all write operations as they happen. After applying an insert, update, or delete operation to the database (2), the application server therefore sends an a fully[3] specified representation of the written database object to InvaliDB. By matching every incoming write against all active real-time queries, InvaliDB is able to compute and emit incremental change deltas (3) that subscribed clients use to update their local state: By default, InvaliDB piggybacks the initial query result to the acknowledgment message delivered upfront and sends out incremental changes in addition every time the result changes.

---

[3]Unlike Meteor's oplog tailing which may receive incomplete write data (cf. p. 27), InvaliDB therefore does not require database access for real-time query maintenance.

Two-Dimensional Workload Partitioning for Linear Scalability

Unlike all other real-time databases currently available, Baqend's real-time query
engine scales with both read and write workload at the same time. To enable higher
write throughput and more concurrent real-time queries than a single machine
could handle, InvaliDB hash-partitions both real-time queries and incoming write
operations evenly across a cluster of machines: By assigning each node in the cluster
to exactly one **query partition** and exactly one **write partition**, any given node is
only responsible for only a subset of all queries and just a fraction of all written data
items.

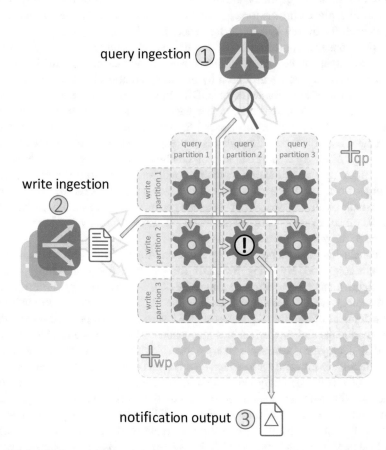

Fig. 3.6 InvaliDB partitions real-time query workload by both queries and incoming write
operations, so that any given matching node is only responsible for matching few queries against
some of the writes

    Figure 3.6 depicts an InvaliDB cluster with three query partitions (vertical
blocks) and three write partitions (horizontal blocks). When a subscription request is

received by one of the **query ingestion nodes** (1), it is forwarded to every matching node in the corresponding query partition; while the query itself is broadcasted to all partition members, the items in the initial result are delivered according to their respective write partitions. Likewise, any written database object is received by one of the **write ingestion nodes** (2) and delivered to all nodes in the corresponding write partition. In the example, a change notification is generated by the **matching node** (3) that is responsible for the intersection of query partition 2 and write partition 2. To detect result changes, every matching node matches any incoming after-image against all of its queries and compares the current against the former matching status of the corresponding object. Since every matching node only holds a subset of all active queries and only maintains a partition of the corresponding query results, processing or storage limitations of an individual node do not become a bottleneck for overall system performance: By adding query partitions ($+_{qp}$) or write partitions ($+_{wp}$), the number of sustainable active queries and overall system write throughput can be increased, respectively. In similar fashion, the sustainable rate of data intake can be increased by providing additional nodes for query and write stream ingestion. Baqend's InvaliDB implementation adheres to the syntax and semantics of MongoDB's query language for sorted filter queries over single collections, with limit and offset clauses.[4] In more detail, it supports query operators for content-based filtering through regular expressions ($regex), comparisons (e.g. $eq, $ne, $gt, $gte), logical combination of filter expressions (e.g. $and, $or, $not), evaluating matching conditions over array values (e.g. $in, $elemMatch, $all, $size), and various others (e.g. $exists, $mod). Real-time variants of full-text search ($text) and geo queries (e.g. $geoIntersects, $geoWithin, $nearSphere) are being evaluated internally, but have not been released to the public at the time of writing.

In conclusion, Baqend provides expressive real-time queries with high scalability and fault tolerance. By using InvaliDB for real-time query matching, Baqend implements a strict **separation of concerns** between the primary storage system and the subsystem for real-time features. Thus, Baqend effectively decouples the failure domains of traditional pull-based OLTP workloads and push-based real-time query workloads and further enables independent scaling for both. Since a single InvaliDB deployment can serve many application servers, Baqend's architecture further facilitates efficient multi-tenant deployments where many applications share resources for real-time query matching to mitigate load spikes and minimize costs per tenant. Since an application server essentially serves as just a message broker in this setup, serving real-time queries has little impact on application server performance. Since InvaliDB can sustain extreme workloads through its unique workload partitioning scheme [Win18, Sec. 4.4], a single Baqend application server is thus able to serve thousands of concurrent real-time queries under thousands of writes per second [Win18, Sec. 5.5.1] [Ges+17, Sec. 6.3]. In similar fashion,

---

[4]For a discussion of how support for real-time aggregations and real-time join queries can be implemented with InvaliDB, see [Win18, Sec. 3.3.2].

Baqend's real-time query mechanism puts minimal load on the underlying storage system, because querying the database is only required for the first subscription for a given real-time query; serving an additional subscription to an already-active real-time query only imposes messaging overhead on the application server and no database interaction whatsoever.

3.3.6   Further Systems

Above, we covered the most expressive real-time databases currently available. In the following, we will briefly survey push-based query mechanisms in other (NoSQL) data storage systems.

Realm [Rea18] is an embedded database often compared with SQLite that provides cross-device synchronization and collection-based real-time queries, both in the form of event stream queries and self-maintaining queries [Rea17]. Write operations are executed locally and synchronized with the *Realm Object Server* which broadcasts them to all clients [RRM17]. Since every client replicates the entire database, reads are always executed locally as well and return very fast. At the same time, however, this scheme introduces the client—e.g. a notebook, tablet, or mobile phone—as a bottleneck for processing as well as storage and the Object Server as a bottleneck for change propagation. In consequence, Realm's real-time queries are only feasible in domains with small data sets and low update throughput. **RxDB** [RxD18] is another embedded database that provides real-time queries through local change detection [Rxdb, Rxda]. It is written in JavaScript and supports different storage backends, using their respective replication protocol to synchronize data from the backend to the client. Like Realm, RxDB is only feasible in scenarios where change monitoring can be handled by the (mobile) client device. **OrientDB** [Ori18] allows filtering newly written objects by a query predicate through so-called Live Queries. Semantically, they appear somewhat collection-based, since they handle inserts, updates, and deletes. But in contrast to systems like Meteor, OrientDB's Live Queries only react to ongoing write operations and do not deliver initially matching items [Del15]. To maintain an up-to-date query result, it is therefore necessary to combine the pull-based query mechanism for the initial result with the push-based mechanism for updates. Self-maintaining queries are thus only possible with custom code. **CouchDB** [Apa18d] is another contender that has an API for continuous changes [ALS10, Ch. 20]. As in OrientDB, the initial result of a query has to be requested separately from the stream of changes. In contrast to many systems discussed in this chapter, though, CouchDB only pushes matching items to the client, i.e. the client will not receive delete notifications.[5] In consequence, self-maintaining queries are complex to implement and require the client to maintain query state. Similar to OrientDB's Live Queries, **Graphcool**

---

[5]The same applies to CouchDB's commercial derivative Cloudant [Clo].

[Gra18] subscriptions filter the write stream by custom criteria. As with OrientDB's Live Queries, the matching process does not consider a query result, but only the data item that is being written [BMS17]. As another similarity, Graphcool subscriptions also do not provide the initially matching items [BM+17]. **Rapid.io** [STR18] is a proprietary database service that provides push-based real-time queries with collection-based semantics, similar to Firestore [Dro17]. As of September 2017, Rapid.io is officially in public Beta and the technology stack behind the query API is undisclosed. Since we are not aware of any case studies or customer reports, we thus cannot set its performance or scalability in perspective to that of the other systems discussed here. Filter queries with comparisons, prefix and suffix matching, and containment checks are supported and can be composed using logical AND/OR; however, it is not possible to use negations or more sophisticated search operators (e.g. regex predicates, wildcards, or case-insensitive search) [Rap]. **Elasticsearch** [Ela18] is a distributed NoSQL database most famously known for its sophisticated full-text search capabilities. Through so-called *percolator queries* [Ban11, Gro16], Elasticsearch supports push-based access in the sense that clients receive notifications as soon as new matches to their queries are written to the database. However, only new matches are registered and no notifications are sent for documents that are deleted or cease matching after an update. Lastly, real-time APIs for **MongoDB** [Mon18a] and **Stitch** [Mon18b, Dan17], a cloud backend by the MongoDB creators, have been introduced in 2017 [Mon17]. However, only stream-based filtering semantics are supported, i.e. updates that remove data from the result cannot be detected [Dav17a, Dav17b].

3.4 Summary and Discussion

Table 3.1 sums up the capabilities of each system detailed in this chapter.

Meteor is the only system featuring two different real-time query implementations: Poll-and-diff scales with write throughput and oplog tailing scales with the number of concurrent real-time queries—neither scales with both. RethinkDB and Parse provide real-time queries with mechanisms similar to oplog tailing and therefore also collapse under heavy write load: The lack of write stream partitioning represents a scale-prohibitive bottleneck in the designs of all these systems. While the technology stack behind Firebase is not disclosed, hard scalability limits for both write throughput and parallel client connections are documented. Further, it is apparent that Firebase mitigates scalability issues by simply denying complex queries to begin with: In the original Firebase model, composite queries are impossible and sorted queries are only allowed with single-attribute ordering keys. Even the more advanced Firestore queries lack support for disjunction of filter expressions (logical OR) and only provide limited options for filter conjunction (logical AND). Because of its unique two-dimensional workload partitioning scheme, Baqend is the only system able to master high write throughput and many concurrent real-time queries at the same time.

Apart from Firebase, all systems in the comparison offer composite filter conditions for real-time queries, but differ in their support for ordered results: Meteor and Baqend support sorted real-time queries with limit and offset, RethinkDB only supports limit (but no offset), and Parse does not support sorting for real-time queries whatsoever. Real-time joins and aggregations are not supported by any current real-time database without query processing at the client (e.g. by computing aggregations or performing the join in application code). All systems covered in the comparison matrix provide an event stream query interface, but only Meteor and Baqend provide interfaces for self-maintaining queries that hide the complexity of handling change deltas from the client.

Table 3.1 A direct comparison of the different real-time query implementations detailed in this chapter

	Meteor		RethinkDB	Parse	Firebase	Baqend
	Poll-and-Diff	Oplog Tailing				
Scales With Write Throughput	✓	✗	✗	✗	✗	✓
Scales With Number of Queries	✗	✓	✓	✓	O (100k connections)	✓
Composite Queries (AND/OR)	✓	✓	✓	✓	O (AND in Firestore)	✓
Sorted Queries	✓	✓	✓	✗	O (single attribute)	✓
Limit	✓	✓	✓	✗	✓	✓
Offset	✓	✓	✗	✗	O (value-based)	✓
Joins	✗	✗	✗	✗	✗	✗
Aggregations	✗	✗	✗	✗	✗	✗
Self-Maintaining Queries	✓	✓	✗	✗	✗	✓
Event Stream Queries	✓	✓	✓	✓	✓	✓

Summing up, most real-time database systems introduce severe compromises in their attempts to carry non-trivial pull-based query features to the push-based paradigm: Since all but one scale only with either the number of clients or with write workload, developers often have to weigh a lack of expressiveness against the presence of hard scalability bottlenecks.

References

[AH98]   Sten F. Andler and Jörgen Hansson, eds. *Active, Real-Time, and Temporal Database Systems*. Lecture Notes in Computer Science 1553. Springer Berlin Heidelberg, 1998.

[ALS10]   J. Chris Anderson, Jan Lehnardt, and Noah Slater. CouchDB: *The Definitive Guide*. 1st. O'Reilly Media, Inc., 2010. ISBN: 0596155891, 9780596155896.

[Bad09]   Antonio Badia. "Quantifiers in Action: Generalized Quantification in Query, Logical and Natural Languages". In: ed. by Ahmed K. Elmagarmid and Amit P. Sheth. Boston, MA: Springer US, 2009. Chap. Extensions, pp. 127–147. ISBN: 978-0-387-09564-6. DOI: 10.1007/978-0-387-09564-6_9. URL: https://doi.org/10.1007/978-0-387-09564-6_9.

[Bak+11] Jason Baker et al. "Megastore: Providing Scalable, for Interactive Services." In: *CIDR*. Vol. 11. 2011, pp. 223–234. (Visited on 12/19/2014).

[Ban11]   Shay Banon. "Percolator". In: *Elastic Blog* (Feb. 2011). Accessed: 2017-11-17. URL: https://www.elastic.co/blog/percolator.

[Baq18]   Baqend. *Baqend*. Accessed: 2018-05-10. 2018. URL: https://www.baqend.com/.

[BM+17]   Nikolas Burk, Nilan Marktanner, et al. "GraphQL vs. Firebase". In: *Graphcool Docs* (2017). Accessed: 2017-07-18. URL: https://www.graph.cool/docs/tutorials/graphql-vs-firebasechi6oozus1/.

[BMS17]   Nikolas Burk, Nilan Marktanner, and Johannes Schickling. "How to build a Real-Time Chat with GraphQL Subscriptions and Apollo?" In: *Graphcool Docs* (2017). Accessed: 2017-07-18. URL: https://www.graph.cool/docs/tutorials/worldchat-subscriptionsexample-ui0eizishe/.

[Bov17]   Pier Bover. "Firebase: the great, the meh, and the ugly". In: *freeCode-Camp Blog* (Jan. 2017). Accessed: 2017-05-21. URL: https://medium.freecodecamp.com/firebase-the-great-the-meh-and-the-ugly-a07252fbcf15.

[Clo]   *Cloudant NoSQL DB Docs: Filter Functions*. Accessed: 2018-05-2. IBM. May 2018. URL: https://console.bluemix.net/docs/services/Cloudant/api/design_documents.html#filter-functions.

[Col16]   Tom Coleman. "The Oplog Observe Driver". In: *Meteor Documentation* (2016). Accessed: 2017-10-16. URL: https://github.com/meteor/docs/blob/cc3f8fe99b3db72c21ea2c0e8d7e574bca860ec6/long-form/oplog-observe-driver.md.

[Dan17]   Eric Daniels. "MongoDB Stitch - Backend as a Service (commentary)". In: *Hacker News* (2017). Accessed 2017-11-17. URL: https://news.ycombinator.com/item?id=14595456.

[Dav17a] A. Jesse Jiryu Davis. "New Driver Features for MongoDB 3.6 (commentary)". In: *emptysquare Blog* (Oct. 2017). Accessed: 2017-11-17. URL: https://emptysqua.re/blog/driver-featuresfor-mongodb-3-6/#comment-3574381334.

[Dav17b] A. Jesse Jiryu Davis. "New Driver Features for MongoDB 3.6: Notification API". In: *emptysquare Blog* (June 2017). Accessed: 2018-04-23. URL: https://emptysqua.re/blog/driver-featuresfor-mongodb-3-6/.

[Del15]   Luigi Dell'Aquila. "LiveQuery". In: *OrientDB Blog* (Oct. 2015). Accessed: 2017-07-09. URL: http://orientdb.com/livequery/.

[Dro17]   David Drobik. "Will Google Build Your Product?" In: *David Drobik – Blog* (Oct. 2017). Accessed: 2017-12-23. URL: https://medium.com/@daviddrobik/will-google-build-your-product-56508d19524a.

[Duf17]   Alex Dufetel. "Introducing Cloud Firestore: Our New Document Database for Apps". In: *Firebase Blog* (Oct. 2017). Accessed: 2017-12-19. URL: https://firebase.googleblog.com/2017/10/introducing-cloud-firestore.html.

[Ela18]   Elasticsearch. *Elasticsearch*. Accessed: 2018-05-10. 2018. URL: https://www.elastic.co/products/elasticsearch/.

[Eri98] Joakim Eriksson. "Real-Time and Active Databases: A Survey". In: *Active, Real-Time, and Temporal Database Systems: Second International Workshop, ARTDB-97 Como, Italy, September 8–9, 1997 Proceedings*. Ed. by Sten F. Andler and Jörgen Hansson. Berlin, Heidelberg: Springer Berlin Heidelberg, 1998, pp. 1–23. ISBN: 978-3-540-49151-4. DOI: 10.1007/3-540-49151-1_1. URL: http://dx.doi.org/10.1007/3-540-49151-1_1.

[Fira] *Choose a Database: Cloud Firestore or Realtime Database*. Accessed: 2017-12-19. Firebase. Dec. 2017. URL: https://firebase.google.com/docs/firestore/rtdb-vs-firestore.

[Firb] Firestore: *Quotas and Limits*. Accessed: 2017-12-19. Firebase. Dec. 2017. URL: https://firebase.google.com/docs/firestore/quotas.

[Firc] *Order and Limit Data with Cloud Firestore*. Accessed: 2017-12-19. Firebase. Dec. 2017. URL: https://firebase.google.com/docs/firestore/query-data/order-limit-data.

[Fird] *Perform Simple and Compound Queries in Cloud Firestore*. Accessed: 2017-12-19. Firebase. Dec. 2017. URL: https://firebase.google.com/docs/firestore/query-data/queries.

[Fire] *Realtime Database Limits*. Accessed: 2017-11-17. Firebase. Nov. 2017. URL: https://firebase.google.com/docs/database/usage/limits.

[Fir16] Firebase. *Firebase*. Accessed: 2016-09-18. 2016. URL: https://firebase.google.com/.

[Fir17] Firebase. "Best practices for data structure: Avoid nesting data". In: *Firebase Docs* (2017). Accessed: 2017-05-21. URL: https://firebase.google.com/docs/database/web/structure-data#avoid_nesting_data.

[Ges+17] Felix Gessert et al. "Quaestor: Query Web Caching for Database-as-a-Service Providers". In: *Proceedings of the 43rd International Conference on Very Large Data Bases* (2017).

[Ges17] Felix Gessert. "The AWS and MongoDB Infrastructure of Parse: Lessons Learned". In: *Baqend Tech Blog* (Jan. 2017). Accessed: 2017-11-29. URL: https://medium.baqend.com/parse-is-gone-afew-secrets-about-their-infrastructure-91b3ab2fcf71.

[Goo18] Google. *Google Cloud Datastore*. Accessed: 2018-05-10. 2018. URL: https://cloud.google.com/datastore/.

[Gro16] Martijn van Groningen. "Elasticsearch Percolator Continues to Evolve". In: *Elastic Blog* (June 2016). Accessed: 2017-11-17. URL: https://www.elastic.co/blog/elasticsearch-percolatorcontinues-to-evolve.

[Jam16] Baptiste Jamin. "Reasons Not To Use Firebase". In: *Chris Blog* (Sept. 2016). Accessed: 2017-05-21. URL: https://crisp.im/blog/why-you-should-never-use-firebase-realtime-database/.

[Kat+15] Jacob Katzen et al. *Oplog tailing too far behind not helping*. Accessed: 2017-07-09. 2015. URL: https://forums.meteor.com/t/oplog-tailing-too-far-behind-not-helping/2235.

[Ker17] Todd Kerpelman. "Cloud Firestore for Realtime Database Developers". In: *Firebase Blog* (Oct. 2017). Accessed: 2017-12-23. URL: https://firebase.googleblog.com/2017/10/cloud-firestorefor-rtdb-developers.html.

[Lac16] Kevin Lacker. "Moving On". In: *Parse Blog* (Jan. 2016). Accessed: 2017-11-18. URL: http://blog.parseplatform.org/announcements/moving-on/.

[Leh14] Michael Lehenbauer. "Firebase: Now with more querying!" In: *Firebase Blog* (Nov. 2014). Accessed: 2017-12-23. URL: https://firebase.googleblog.com/2014/11/firebase-now-with-morequerying.html.

[Mao+14] Andrew Mao et al. *My experience hitting limits on Meteor performance*. Accessed: 2017-07-09. 2014. URL: https://groups.google.com/forum/#!topic/meteor-talk/Y547Hh2z39Y.

[Mar15] Watts Martin. "Changefeeds in RethinkDB". In: *RethinkDB Docs* (2015). Accessed: 2017-07-09. URL: https://rethinkdb.com/docs/changefeeds/javascript/#changefeeds-with-filteringand-aggregation-queries.

[Mar16] Watts Martin. "Table joins in RethinkDB". In: *RethinkDB Docs* (2016). Accessed: 2017-11-17. URL: https://www.rethinkdb.com/docs/table-joins/.

[Mew16]   Daniel Mewes. "Scaling, sharding and replication: Running a proxy node". In: *RethinkDB Docs* (2016). Accessed: 2017-07-09. URL: https://rethinkdb.com/docs/sharding-and-replication/#running-a-proxy-node.

[Mon]   *MongoDB CRUD Concepts: Tailable Cursor.* Accessed: 2017-11-13. MongoDB Inc. 2017. URL: https://docs.mongodb.com/manual/core/tailable-cursors/.

[Puf16]   Frank van Puffelen. "Have you met the Realtime Database?" In: *Firebase Blog* (July 2016). Accessed: 2017-05-20. URL: https://firebase.googleblog.com/2016/07/have-you-met-realtimedatabase.html.

[Pur+93] B. Purimetla et al. *A Study of Distributed Real-Time Active Database Applications.* Tech. rep. Amherst, MA, USA, 1993.

[Rap]   *Rapid Docs: Collection.* Accessed: 2017-10-06. STRV s.r.o. 2017. URL: https://www.rapidrealtime.com/docs/api-reference/javascript/collection.

[Rea17]   Realm. "Realm Java 3.0: Collection Notifications, Snapshots and Sorting Across Relationships". In: *Realm Blog* (Feb. 2017). Accessed: 2017-07-09. URL: https://news.realm.io/news/realm-java-3-0-collection-notifications/.

[Rea18]   Realm. *Realm.* Accessed: 2018-05-10. 2018. URL: https://realm.io/.

[Ret16]   RethinkDB. *RethinkDB.* Accessed: 2016-09-18. 2016. URL: https://www.rethinkdb.com/.

[Ric13]   Kato Richardson. "Queries, Part 1: Common SQL Queries Converted for Firebase". In: *Firebase Blog* (Oct. 2013). Accessed: 2017-12-23. URL: https://firebase.googleblog.com/2013/10/queries-part-1-common-sql-queries.html.

[Ric14]   Kato Richardson. "Queries, Part 2: Advanced Searches with Firebase, made Plug-and-Play Simple". In: *Firebase Blog* (Jan. 2014). Accessed: 2017-12-23. URL: https://firebase.googleblog.com/2014/10/firebase-is-joining-google.html.

[Ros11]   Ian Thomas Rose. "Real-Time Query Systems for Complex Data Sources". PhD thesis. Harvard University Cambridge, Massachusetts, 2011.

[Ros16]   Alex Rose. "Firebase: The Good, Bad, and the Ugly". In: *Raizlabs Developer Blog* (Dec. 2016). Accessed: 2017-05-21. URL: https://www.raizlabs.com/dev/2016/12/firebase-case-study/.

[RRM17]   Nic Raboy, Priya Rajagopal, and Eric Maxwell. "NDP Episode #19: Mobile Development with Realm". In: *Couchbase Blog* (June 2017). audio podcast (explanation by Eric Maxwell, starting at 10:57); Accessed: 2017-09-13. URL: https://blog.couchbase.com/ndp-episode-19-mobile-development-realm/.

[Rxda]   *Custom Build.* Accessed: 2017-10-16. RxDB. 2017. URL: https://pubkey.github.io/rxdb/custom-build.html.

[Rxdb]   *Query Change Detection.* Accessed: 2017-10-16. RxDB. 2017. URL: https://pubkey.github.io/rxdb/query-change-detection.html.

[RxD18]   RxDB. *RxDB.* Accessed: 2018-05-10. 2018. URL: https://github.com/pubkey/rxdb.

[San18]   Salvatore Sanfilippo. *Redis.* Accessed: 2018-05-10. 2018. URL: https://redis.io/.

[SF12]   Pramod J. Sadalage and Martin Fowler. *NoSQL Distilled: A Brief Guide to the Emerging World of Polyglot Persistence.* 1st. Addison-Wesley Professional, 2012. ISBN: 0321826620, 9780321826626.

[Sta88]   John A. Stankovic. "Misconceptions About Real-Time Computing: A Serious Problem for Next-Generation Systems". In: *Computer* 21.10 (Oct. 1988), pp. 10–19. ISSN: 0018–9162. DOI: 10.1109/2.7053. URL: http://dx.doi.org/10.1109/2.7053.

[Ste17]   William Stein. "RethinkDB versus PostgreSQL: my personal experience". In: *CoCalc Blog* (Feb. 2017). Accessed: 2017-07-09. URL: https://blog.sagemath.com/2017/02/09/rethinkdb-vspostgres.html.

[Tam14]   James Tamplin. "Firebase is Joining Google!" In: *Firebase Blog* (Oct. 2014). Accessed: 2017-11-17. URL: https://firebase.googleblog.com/2014/10/firebase-is-joining-google.html.

[Tam16]   James Tamplin. "Firebase expands to become a unified app platform". In: *Firebase Blog* (May 2016). Accessed: 2017-12-23. URL: https://firebase.googleblog.com/2016/05/firebase-expands-to-become-unified-app-platform.html.

[Tam17]   James Tamplin. "Cloud Firestore: A New Document Database for Apps (commentary)". In: *Hacker News* (2017). Accessed 2017-12-19. URL: https://news.ycombinator.com/item?id=15393499.

[Tos+14] Ankit Toshniwal et al. "Storm@Twitter". In: *Proceedings of the 2014 ACM SIGMOD International Conference on Management of Data*. SIGMOD'14. Snowbird, Utah, USA: ACM, 2014, pp. 147–156. ISBN: 978-1-4503-2376-5. DOI: 10.1145/2588555.2595641. URL: http://doi.acm.org/10.1145/2588555.2595641.

[TS+09]   Lawrence To, Viv Schupmann, et al. *Oracle Database High Availability Best Practices 11g Release 1 (11.1)*. Accessed: 2017-05-13. Oracle. Dec. 2009. URL: https://docs.oracle.com/cd/B28359_01/server.111/b28282/glossary.htm#CHDIDADC.

[Wan16a] MengyanWang. "Parse LiveQuery Protocol Specification". In: *GitHub: ParsePlatform/parse-server* (Mar. 2016). Accessed: 2017-11-18. URL: https://github.com/parse-community/parse-server/wiki/Parse-LiveQuery-Protocol-Specification.

[Wan16b] Mengyan Wang. "Parse Server Goes Realtime with Live Queries". In: *Parse Blog* (Mar. 2016). Accessed: 2017-11-18. URL: http://blog.parseplatform.org/announcements/parse-server-goes-realtime-with-live-queries/.

[Wen15]   Jacob Wenger. "List chat group in order of most recently posted". In: *Firebase Google Group* (June 2015). Accessed: 2017-07-09. URL: https://groups.google.com/forum/#!msg/firebase-talk/d-XjaBVL2Ko/TmkIep44lGgJ.

[Win18]   Wolfram Wingerath. "Scalable Push-Based Real-Time Queries on Top of Pull-Based Databases". PhD thesis. University of Hamburg, 2019. URL: https://invalidb.info/thesis.

[Wor+14] David Workman et al. "Large number of operations hangs server". In: *Meteor GitHub Issues* (2014). Accessed: 2016-10-01. URL: https://github.com/meteor/meteor/issues/2668.

[Apa18d] Apache Software Foundation. *CouchDB*. Accessed: 2018-05-10. 2018. URL: http://couchdb.apache.org/.

[CoC18]   CoCalc by SageMath, Inc. *CoCalc*. Accessed: 2018-05-10. 2018. URL: https://cocalc.com/.

[Gra18]   Graphcool, Inc. *Graphcool*. Accessed: 2018-05-10. 2018. URL: https://www.graph.cool/.

[Met15]   Meteor Development Group. "Livequery". In: *Meteor Change Log v1.0.4* (Mar. 2015). Accessed: 2017-07-09. URL: http://docs.meteor.com/changelog.html#livequery-1.

[Met16]   Meteor Development Group. "Tuning Meteor Mongo Livedata for Scalability". In: *Meteor Blog* (May 2016). Accessed: 2017-05-12. URL: https://blog.meteor.com/tuning-meteor-mongolivedata-for-scalability-13fe9deb8908.

[Met18]   Meteor Development Group. *Meteor*. Accessed: 2018-05-10. 2018. URL: https://www.meteor.com/.

[Mon17]   MongoDB Inc. "MongoDB 3.6.0-rc0 is released". In: *MongoDB Blog* (Oct. 2017). Accessed: 2017-11-17. URL: https://www.mongodb.com/blog/post/mongodb-360-rc0-is-released.

[Mon18a] MongoDB Inc. *MongoDB*. Accessed: 2018-05-10. 2018. URL: https://www.mongodb.com.

[Mon18b] MongoDB Inc. *MongoDB Stitch*. Accessed: 2018-05-10. 2018. URL: https://mongodb.com/cloud/stitch.

[Ori18]   OrientDB Ltd. *OrientDB*. Accessed: 2018-05-10. 2018. URL: https://orientdb.com/.

[STR18]   STRV s.r.o. *Rapid – Realtime Database Services*. Accessed: 2018-05-10. 2018. URL: https://www.rapidrealtime.com/.

Chapter 4
Data Stream Management

In some domains, data arrives so fast and in such great quantity that storing it in a database collection is simply infeasible [Bab+02]. When the incoming data relates to ongoing (real-world) events that require immediate action, persistence may further not even be useful; for example, data in electronic trading, network monitoring, or real-time fraud detection is only valuable for a short amount of time and therefore has to be utilized immediately [SCZ05]. To adapt to these circumstances, data stream management systems (DSMSs) introduce the **data stream** as an abstraction for an infinite sequence of database records that arrive over time. The raw data streams arriving at the systems are usually referred to as *base streams*, whereas those resulting from data transformations (e.g. queries) are called *derived streams* [GZ10]. Since a data stream is impossible to store entirely due to its unbounded nature, DSMSs drop the database requirement of eternal data persistence: They retain incoming records for limited time only and eventually discard them.

4.1 Queries Over Streams

Queries over streams are long-running and produce new output whenever new data is received; this is in contrast to ad hoc queries over collections which produce output once on user request. Thus, queries over streams generate output streams, just like queries over database relations produce output relations (i.e. result lists). In spite of these fundamental differences between queries over collections and queries over streams, however, streaming query languages are usually designed to resemble traditional database languages: While some systems for stream management expose procedural interfaces (e.g. Aurora [Aba+03, Car+02] or Borealis [Aba+05]), most systems employ SQL-like query languages that extend relational algebra through special operators for handling streams (e.g. STREAM [ABW06], Tapestry [Ter+92], TelegraphCQ [Cha+03], PipelineDB [Nel17], S-Store [Cet+14]); in fact, several DSMSs are built on top of pull-based databases (e.g. TelegraphCQ and PipelineDB extend PostgreSQL, S-store extends H-Store [Kal+08]). Therefore, data streams are often implemented as **time-varying collections** [GZ10, Sec. 2.3.1] where new records are inserted and old records are deleted (cf. PipelineDB [Pipa] and S-store [Cet+14, Sec. 3.2.1]).

Early systems (e.g. Tapestry) only supported **append-only** streams, i.e. they relied on the assumption that records are only added and never modified or removed. When tuples represent sensor measurements or other unchangeable facts, this assumption is valid; in fact, base stream data is final in most applications [GZ10, Sec. 2.1.1]. Query results are commonly not immutable, though, since they can evolve over time; as an example, consider a query that collects the maximum temperature of the day from a feed of sensor readings. To accommodate such non-monotonic data sources, modern DSMSs are developed with support for **mutable streams** where issued data can be revised [Ryv+06, GAE06, Gha+07]: Queries over streams in these systems can be used to maintain predicate-based relations up-to-date, similar to materialized views. Some DSMS query implementations even bear resemblance to the real-time query mechanisms discussed in Chap. 3. For example, *insert/delete streams* in STREAM [ABW06, Sec. 6.3] and *delta streams* in PipelineDB [Nel17] produce change deltas similar to event stream queries. As another example, *relation streams* in STREAM [ABW06, Sec. 6.3] [BSW04] produce fully maintained results very much like self-maintaining queries do.

It is important to note, though, that DSMSs and real-time databases operate on differently scoped data sets: Since DSMSs do not retain data indefinitely, queries over streams only reflect recent data whereas queries in a real-time database reflect all data that ever entered the system. By intuition, this means that DSMSs essentially access data that is yet to arrive, because old portions of the stream are oftentimes not available anymore. In consequence, queries over streams in DSMSs do not behave like collection-based real-time queries unless they are defined over **monotonic or quasi-monotonic attributes**[1] and only refer to recent data. Queries that reference non-monotonic attributes (e.g. username) can only produce output from the currently buffered portion of the stream; data that has been discarded is effectively lost for queries to come. Therefore, use of non-monotonic attributes for queries over streams is sometimes forbidden (see for example Calcite [Cal]).

---

[1]An attribute is *monotonic*, if all its values are either decreasing or increasing, such as arrival timestamps in a centralized DSMS. Similarly, an attribute is *quasi-monotonic*, if it is correlated to a monotonic attribute. For example, the time at which an event is registered according to a sensor's local clock (event time) is quasi-monotonic, because it typically corresponds to the time at which it is received according to the server's clock (arrival time) within a certain error margin (cf. Sect. 4.2).

```
                                         SELECT name
      SELECT name                          FROM Users
        FROM Users                        WHERE timestamp > now()
```

(a) This query cannot be answered without knowledge of the entire data stream.

(b) This query explicitly and exclusively refers to future information and can therefore be processed based on the stream alone.

Listing 4.1 Whether or not a query can be answered on the basis of an ephemeral data stream without access to the stream history depends on the temporal scope of the query

For illustration, consider a data management system receiving a stream of user actions as presented in Sect. 1.3. If the data management system is a DSMS, it disposes of data after a while and therefore is only aware of users that have been active recently. A real-time database, on the other hand, would be aware of all users, because it maintains a persistent data repository that reflects the entire data stream. This point is illustrated by the queries in Listing 4.1: A complete list of all registered users (a) can only be produced by the real-time database, because the DSMS does not have access to all relevant data as soon as the first portion of the stream has been discarded. If the result is constrained to current and future users (b), however, the query result can be computed by the real-time database and the DSMS alike, because it does not require historical knowledge of the stream.

Several DSMSs account for the need to access historical data by letting users combine queries over unbounded data streams with queries over persistent database collections. While this enables both query types illustrated in Listing 4.1, executing stream queries without bounded windows is often considered infeasible for practical workloads (cf. [Wid05]) as scalability of database-rooted DSMSs is typically limited. STREAM, for example, is a centralized DSMS that does not scale horizontally at all [Ara+16, Sec. 8.1], while PipelineDB does not support data sharding (i.e. every node maintains the entire data set) and is only able to distribute query processing across few nodes because of synchronization overhead for replication.[2] For systems that are not built on databases, achieving query semantics as illustrated above can further be difficult, because their query languages are sometimes hardly comparable with traditional database languages such as SQL.[3]

---

[2] All write operations in PipelineDB are coordinated synchronously via two-phase commit between all nodes [Pipb], so that highly distributed setups are likely to experience increased latency as well as reduced throughput and availability [Pan15, Sec. 3.1].

[3] As an example, consider the graphical user interface of Aurora/Borealis which is based on arrows and boxes rather than SQL-style declarative statements [Çet+16].

4.2 Notions of Time

Since records in streams often refer to events in a complex distributed system, they can be attributed with different timestamps. For example, a record may carry the time at which it was received by the DSMS (**arrival time**) and the time at which the corresponding event actually occurred according to the measuring device's local clock (**event time**) [GZ10]. Event and arrival time are usually correlated and ideally close. In practice, however, there is often a delay between the occurrence of an event and its registration in the stream management system. For example, consider user data that is collected on a smart phone and reported sporadically through the Internet; depending on network connectivity, clock skew between the mobile device and the DSMS, and other factors, event time and arrival time for a particular record may diverge by seconds, hours, or even days [Aki15].

Since base streams are naturally ordered by the arrival timestamp, they have to be reorganized whenever application semantics evolve around a different notion of time such as event time. For **stream reordering**, the input stream is buffered for t_Δ time units and items within the buffered portion of the stream are reorganized and emitted according to the sort specification [Aba+03, Sec. 5.2.2]. Records that arrive more than t_Δ time units late are typically dropped from the reordered stream [GZ10, Sec. 2.2.2]. It is also possible to revise stream output on receiving **delayed records** instead of dropping them: The basic idea is to revoke previously issued information (that has turned out to be incorrect) and to emit updated records which reflect the new information [Ryv+06]. However, providing **revised output** takes a performance toll on the upstream component, just like applying revised output can be expensive for downstream components.[4]

Since system performance can degrade significantly when output has to be retained for a long time [ABB+13, Sec. 8.4], different approaches limit the amount of state utilized for compensating out-of-order arrival. Some systems use a fixed value for the time or the number of records to buffer (e.g. Aurora [Aba+03]). Other systems dynamically control the amount of metadata by measuring or estimating the current delay within the application stack (e.g. NiagaraCQ [Che+00], MillWheel [ABB+13], Gigascope [Joh+05]). Special records are used to propagate this kind of information from upstream components further downstream. For example, a **punctuation** [Tuc+03] is a record that carries an invariant condition such as timestamp $\geq$ "12h05m00s" that is guaranteed to be true for all subsequent records; thus, all buffered records that do not fulfill the invariant can be safely abandoned (e.g. all records from before timestamp "12h05m00s"). So-called **heartbeats** [SW04] or **watermarks** [ABB+13] serve a similar purpose. Computing or estimating these invariant conditions, however, is challenging in some settings [SW04].

---

[4]Specifically, providing undo information requires buffering the original output [Aki+15, Sec. 2.3]. Likewise, reprocessing huge amounts of data to generate updated records can lead to CPU contention and can thus significantly impair overall system performance [Kre14c].

4.3 Windowing and Approximation

Queries over streams are usually evaluated in the context of a **window**, i.e. a finite partition of the conceptually unbounded sequence of records. There are several dimensions by which a window can be described [GZ10, Sec. 2.1.2]. One dimension is the **direction** of movement, relating to the way that start and end point of the window are chosen: Either both are fixed (*fixed window*), one is fixed and one is moving (*landmark window*), or both are moving (*sliding window*) [PS06]; windows can also be *expanding* or *contracting*, depending on whether the window boundaries are moving in the same direction or whether they are moving at the same speed. Further, windows can be distinguished by the way their **contents** are defined. Most commonly, window contents are specified in terms of *time* (e.g. "all data from the last two minutes") or *count* (e.g. "the last 1000 records") [ABW06, Sec. 6], but other forms of defining a stream partition are possible, for instance based on query *predicates* [GAE06, Jai+08]. Movement and **update frequency** can also be used to characterize a window. Intuitively, a *sliding window* [Gol06] is eagerly refreshed with every incoming record: The window advances as one record enters and another one leaves. When a new query result is produced lazily every *n* time units or every *n* tuples instead, the window is called a *jumping window* [Ma+05]. When the update interval equals window size, the stream is split into contiguous, non-overlapping ranges. Since these windows are often illustrated to "tumble over" from one range to the next, they are referred to as *tumbling windows*.

In comparison to sliding or jumping windows, tumbling windows are relatively easy to implement, because their **state** is reset on every move: In other words, only new tuples have to be incorporated when updating a tumbling window. Sliding and jumping windows, in contrast, are more complex (and sometimes less efficient) to realize [GZ10], because they have to reflect tuples moving out of the window as well. In consequence, the metadata required for incremental computation of a query result over a sliding window can vary significantly depending on the query type [Feg16]. For example, maintaining a counter is very straightforward, as it is incremented for every new record and decremented for every expiring record; more complex aggregations such as an average, in contrast, may require retaining all records within the window, because their contribution to the query result depends on their concrete values.

To reduce the amount of metadata required for incremental query result computation, specific algorithms and data structures have been developed for the **approximation** of value frequencies [Gib01, PT05, MM02], quantiles [GK01, Lin+04], top-*k* queries [MBP06, DLOM02, GM98, MAEA05b], skyline queries [Lin+05, TP06], aggregate queries [Dat+02, Li+05, GKS01a, CM05], range queries [BL10], and other query types [Dat+02, Fei+03, MAEA05a, GKS01b]. Workloads are further bursty in many streaming applications [Kle02] and therefore input rates may (temporarily) exceed system capacity, despite optimized implementations. In order to prevent system overload in such scenarios, a DSMS may resort to **load shedding** [Tat+03]: Here, the DSMS deliberately skips records within the stream to reduce effective load. There are different strategies for selecting to-be-skipped tuples (e.g. probabilistic sampling [SH12, BDM07] or selection by semantic criteria [AN04]). Which one fits a given scenario best depends on the optimization target (e.g. throughput, quality of service [Mot+03]).

4.4 Complex Event Processing

In some applications, the relevant information may not be explicitly represented in the individual base stream entries, but rather implicitly encoded in the context between them. Systems for **complex event processing (CEP)** [CM12, CVZ13] address these applications by capturing the temporal, local, or even causal relationships and dependencies between individual records. Similar to active databases (cf. Sect. 2.1), CEP systems execute business logic and thus proactively trigger actions; these may range from a simple notification of maintenance personnel to an emergency shutdown of failing hardware [ENL11]. Depending on the concrete system, the **rules** that determine application behavior are either defined through a declarative language, imperative programming, or a graphical user interface [VRR10]. By establishing a **context** between stream entries, CEP systems thus create data streams with a higher level of **abstraction** from the low-level base streams [BD15]. Typical use cases include prediction of customer behavior [Ali+09], monitoring freight logistics [RRH13], routing network traffic in realtime to maximize quality of service [Ara13], and intrusion detection [FR11].

For illustration, consider an array of temperature sensors deployed for monitoring hardware in a data center. Through aggregation and correlation of different readings over time, a CEP engine can derive pieces of information which are more abstract and more relevant to the application domain than the raw temperature values [Pal13]. For example, **complex error conditions** (e.g. machines in a particular rack overheating) might be detected by considering measurements of different sensors over time. Likewise, sensor readings that appear plausible in themselves might be uncovered as faulty when they deviate significantly from output of colocated sensors.

The requirement to correlate events with one another makes CEP engines inherently difficult to scale across machine boundaries [Car+17] and therefore deployments usually do not span more than a few nodes [Esp, IBM14, Pipb]. However, distribution can be achieved by application-level sharding or by building abstraction hierarchies that reduce the number of events to process on every individual machine [BD15, Sec. 2.4]. Since general-purpose stream processing systems (cf. Chap. 5) can also be used for complex event processing and sometimes even provide abstractions to facilitate this task (e.g. Flink [KW17]), the line between complex event processing and general-purpose stream processing has become blurred [Vin16].

4.5   Messaging Middleware

Processing streaming data in a massively distributed system necessitates funneling information from the system periphery into a data stream and propagating it with low latency. In contrast to systems for change data capture (cf. Sect. 2.2), **message-oriented middleware (MOM)** is not primarily concerned with collecting relevant information on events as they occur, but mainly implements efficient and often reliable mechanisms for data distribution: A **producer** provides data items to the messaging middleware which then delivers them to one or many **consumers**. Various forms of propagation are common, for example *point-to-point* (single producer, single consumer) or *publish-subscribe* (single producer, multiple consumers) delivery. The provided delivery guarantees range from none (e.g. publish-subscribe in Redis [San18] or NATS [Nat]) over at-least-once (e.g. in Kafka [KNR11]) to exactly-once (e.g. RabbitMQ [Piv18], ActiveMQ [Apa18a], Qpid [Apa18f], HornetQ [Gia12], or IBM WebSphere MQ [Lam+12]). In order to acknowledge individual messages, some MOMs keep track of each consumer's delivery log and retain messages that have not been acknowledged by all consumers. When implemented in this fashion, exactly-once delivery may incur significant overhead and can even bring the entire system down when just one single consumer stays disconnected for a long time. To avoid this kind of failure scenario, **distributed log systems** such as Kafka archive all data to disk and allow clients to request data replays by providing a log offset of event history. Thus, data can be retained for days or even weeks with minimal processing overhead for the middleware, while *at-least*-once delivery guarantees are naturally met through the ability to replay the archived messages. *Exactly*-once delivery guarantees are still achievable, but at the cost of reduced scalability [Tre15, Tre17] and/or significantly increased system complexity [Nar17]. While simple content-based and even rule-based filtering is supported by some systems (e.g. Siena [CRW01] or Delta [KKM13]), querying capability is typically limited in comparison to the systems discussed above.

4.6   Summary and Discussion

Data stream management systems are similar to real-time databases in several ways. First, they support continuous queries, i.e. they proactively deliver information as soon as new data of relevance becomes available. Second, many of them are also capable of ad hoc queries over currently buffered data; in fact, many data stream management systems are extensions of existing databases and therefore inherit some of their capabilities. As an important distinction to real-time databases, however, data streams are typically retained for only a relatively short amount of time. Seeing that data stream management systems are thus oriented towards current and future events, querying data that is rooted in the past is inefficient or impossible without a second system for persistent data management.

References

[Aba+03] Daniel J. Abadi et al. "Aurora: A New Model and Architecture for Data Stream Management". In: *The VLDB Journal* 12.2 (Aug. 2003), pp. 120–139. ISSN: 1066–8888. URL: https://doi.org/10.1007/s00778-003-0095-z. http://dx.doi.org/10.1007/s00778-003-0095-z.

[Aba+05] Daniel J Abadi et al. "The Design of the Borealis Stream Processing Engine". In: *Second Biennial Conference on Innovative Data Systems Research (CIDR 2005)*. Asilomar, CA, 2005.

[ABB+13] Tyler Akidau, Alex Balikov, Kaya Bekiroglu, et al. "MillWheel: Fault-Tolerant Stream Processing at Internet Scale". In: *Very Large Data Bases*. 2013, pp. 734–746.

[ABW06] Arvind Arasu, Shivnath Babu, and Jennifer Widom. "The CQL Continuous Query Language: Semantic Foundations and Query Execution". In: *The VLDB Journal* 15.2 (June 2006), pp. 121–142. ISSN: 1066-8888. URL: https://doi.org/10.1007/s00778-004-0147-z. http://dx.doi.org/10.1007/s00778-004-0147-z.

[Aki+15] Tyler Akidau et al. "The Dataflow Model: A Practical Approach to Balancing Correctness, Latency, and Cost in Massive-Scale, Unbounded, Out-of-Order Data Processing". In: *Proceedings of the VLDB Endowment* 8 (2015), pp. 1792–1803.

[Aki15] Tyler Akidau. "The world beyond batch: Streaming 101". In: *O'Reilly Media* (Aug. 2015). Accessed: 2017-05-21. URL: https://www.oreilly.com/ideas/the-world-beyond-batch-streaming-101.

[Ali+09] M.H. Ali et al. "Microsoft CEP Server and Online Behavioral Targeting". In: *Proc. VLDB Endow* 2.2 (Aug. 2009), pp. 1558–1561. ISSN: 2150-8097. URL: https://doi.org/10.14778/1687553.1687590. https://doi.org/10.14778/1687553.1687590.

[AN04] Ahmed M. Ayad and Jeffrey F. Naughton. "Static Optimization of Conjunctive Queries with Sliding Windows over Infinite Streams". In: *Proceedings of the 2004 ACM SIGMOD International Conference on Management of Data* SIGMOD'04. Paris, France: ACM, 2004, pp. 419–430. ISBN: 1-58113-859-8. URL: https://doi.org/10.1145/1007568.1007616. http://doi.acm.org/10.1145/1007568.1007616.

[Ara+16] Arvind Arasu et al. "Data Stream Management: Processing High-Speed Data Streams". In: *Data Stream Management: Processing High-Speed Data Streams*. Ed. by Minos Garofalakis, Johannes Gehrke, and Rajeev Rastogi. Berlin, Heidelberg: Springer Berlin Heidelberg, 2016. Chap. STREAM: The Stanford Data Stream Management System, pp. 317–336. ISBN:978-3-540-28608-0. URL: https://doi.org/10.1007/978-3-540-28608-0_16. https://doi.org/10.1007/978-3-540-28608-0_16.

[Ara13] Mauricio Arango. "Mobile QoS Management Using Complex Event Processing". In: *Proceedings of the 7th ACM International Conference on Distributed Event-based Systems* DEBS' 13. Arlington, Texas, USA: ACM, 2013, pp. 115–122. ISBN: 978-1-4503-1758-0. URL: https://doi.org/10.1145/2488222.2488277. http://doi.acm.org/10.1145/2488222.2488277.

[Bab+02] Brian Babcock et al. "Models and Issues in Data Stream Systems". In: *Proceedings of the Twenty-first ACM SIGMOD-SIGACT-SIGART Symposium on Principles of Database Systems* PODS'02. Madison, Wisconsin: ACM, 2002, pp. 1–16. ISBN: 1-58113-507-6. URL: https://doi.org/10.1145/543613.543615. http://doi.acm.org./10.1145/543613.543615.

[BD15] Ralf Bruns and Jürgen Dunkel. *Complex Event Processing: Komplexe Analyse von massiven Datenströmen mit CEP*. Springer Vieweg, 2015.

[BDM07] Brian Babcock, Mayur Datar, and Rajeev Motwani. "Load Shedding in Data Stream Systems". In: *Data Streams – Models and Algorithms*. Vol. 31. Advances in Database Systems. Springer, 2007, pp. 127–147.

[BL10] Francesco Buccafurri and Gianluca Lax. "Approximating Sliding Windows by Cyclic Tree-like Histograms for Efficient Range Queries". In: *Data Knowl. Eng* 69.9 (Sept. 2010), pp. 979–997. ISSN: 0169-023X. URL: https://doi.org/10.1016/j.datak.2010.5002. http://dx.doi.org/10.1016/j.datak.2010.05.002.

[BSW04] Shivnath Babu, Utkarsh Srivastava, and Jennifer Widom. "Exploiting K-constraints to Reduce Memory Overhead in Continuous Queries over Data Streams". In: *ACM Trans. Database Syst.* 29.3 (Sept. 2004), pp. 545–580. ISSN: 0362-5915. URL: https:// doi.org/10.1145/1016028.1016032. http://doi.acm.org/10.1145/1016028.1016032.

[Cal] *Streaming* Accessed: 2017-11-26. Calcite. Nov 2017. URL: https://calcite.apache.org/ docs/stream.html.

[Car+02] Don Carney et al. "Monitoring Streams: A New Class of Data Management Applications". In: *Proceedings of the 28th International Conference on Very Large Data Bases*. VLDB'02. Hong Kong, China: VLDB Endowment, 2002, pp. 215–226. URL: http://dl.acm.org/citation.cfm?id=1287369.1287389.

[Car+17] Paris Carbone et al. "Large-Scale Data Stream Processing Systems". In: *Handbook of Big Data Technologies*. Springer, 2017, pp. 219–260.

[Cet+14] Ugur Cetintemel et al. "S-Store: A Streaming NewSQL System for Big Velocity Applications". In: *Proc. VLDB Endow* 7.13 (Aug. 2014), pp. 1633–1636. ISSN: 2150- 8097. URL: https://doi.org/10.14778/2733004.2733048. http://dx.doi.org/10.14778/ 2733004.2733048.

[Cha+03] Sirish Chandrasekaran et al. "TelegraphCQ: Continuous Dataflow Processing". In: *Proceedings of the 2003 ACM SIGMOD International Conference on Management of Data* SIGMOD '03. San Diego, California: ACM, 2003, pp. 668–668. ISBN: 1-58113-634-X. URL: https://doi.org/10.1145/872757.872857. http://doi.acm.org/10. 1145/872757.872857.

[Che+00] Jianjun Chen et al. "NiagaraCQ: A Scalable Continuous Query System for Internet Databases". In: *Proceedings of the 2000 ACM SIGMOD International Conference on Management of Data* SIGMOD '00. Dallas, Texas, USA: ACM, 2000, pp. 379– 390. ISBN: 1-58113-217-4. URL: https://doi.org/10.1145/342009.335432. http://doi. acm.org/10.1145/342009.335432.

[CM05] Graham Cormode and S. Muthukrishnan. "An Improved Data Stream Summary: The Count-min Sketch and Its Applications". In: *J. Algorithms* 55.1 (Apr 2005), pp. 58–75. ISSN: 0196-6774. URL: https://doi.org/10.1016/j.jalgor.2003.12.001. http://dxdoiorg/ 10.1016/j.jalgor.2003.12.001

[CM12] Gianpaolo Cugola and Alessandro Margara. "Processing Flows of Information: From Data Stream to Complex Event Processing". In: *ACM Comput. Surv* 44.3 (June 2012), 15:1–15:62. ISSN: 0360-0300. URL: https://doi.org/10.1145/2187671.2187677. http:// doi.acm.org/10.1145/2187671.2187677.

[CRW01] Antonio Carzaniga, David S. Rosenblum, and Alexander L. Wolf. "Design and Evaluation of a Wide-area Event Notification Service". In: *ACM Trans. Comput. Syst.* 19.3 (Aug. 2001), pp. 332–383. ISSN: 0734-2071. URL: https://doi.org/10.1145/ 380749.380767. http://doi.acm.org/10.1145/380749.380767.

[CVZ13] P. Carbone, K. Vandikas, and F Zaloshnja. "Towards Highly Available Complex Event Processing Deployments in the Cloud". In: *2013 Seventh International Conference on Next Generation Mobile Apps, Services and Technologies*. 2013, pp. 153–158. https:// doi.org/10.1109/NGMAST.2013.35

[Dat+02] Mayur Datar et al. "Maintaining Stream Statistics over Sliding Windows". In: *SIAM Journal on Computing* 31.6 (2002), pp. 1794–1813.

[DLOM02] Erik D. Demaine, Alejandro López-Ortiz, and J. Ian Munro. "Frequency Estimation of Internet Packet Streams with Limited Space". In: *Proceedings of the 10th Annual European Symposium on Algorithms*. ESA'02. London, UK, UK: Springer-Verlag, 2002, pp. 348–360. ISBN: 3-540-44180-8. URL: http://dlacmorg/citationcfm? id=647912.740658.

[ENL11] Opher Etzion, Peter Niblett, and David C Luckham. *Event processing in action*. Ed. by Sebastian Stirling. Manning Greenwich, 2011.

[Esp] *How does Esper scale?* Accessed: 2016-09-19. EsperTech. 2016. URL: http://www. espertech.com/esper/faq_esper.php#scaling.

[Feg16] Leonidas Fegaras. "Incremental Query Processing on Big Data Streams". In: *IEEE Trans. on Knowl. and Data Eng.* 28.11 (Nov 2016), pp. 2998–3012. ISSN: 1041-4347. URL: https://doi.org/10.1109/TKDE.2016.2601103. https://doi.org/10.1109/TKDE.2016.2601103.

[Fei+03] Joan Feigenbaum et al. "An Approximate L1-Difference Algorithm for Massive Data Streams". In: *SIAM J Comput.* 32.1 (Jan. 2003), pp. 131–151. ISSN: 0097-5397. URL: https://doi.org/10.1137/S0097539799361701. https://doi.org/10.1137/S0097539799361701.

[FR11] M. Ficco and L. Romano. "A Generic Intrusion Detection and Diagnoser System Based on Complex Event Processing". In: *2011 First International Conference on Data Compression, Communications and Processing* 2011, pp. 275–284. https://doi.org/10.1109/CCP.2011.43.

[GAE06] Thanaa M. Ghanem, Walid G. Aref, and Ahmed K. Elmagarmid. "Ex- ploiting Predicate-window Semantics over Data Streams". In: *SIGMOD Rec.* 35.1 (Mar 2006), pp. 3–8. ISSN: 0163-5808. URL: https://doi.org/10.1145/1121995.1121996. http://doiacmorg/10.1145/1121995.1121996

[Gha+07] T M. Ghanem et al. "Incremental Evaluation of Sliding-Window Queries over Data Streams". In: *IEEE Transactions on Knowledge and Data Engineering* 19.1 (2007), pp. 57–72. ISSN: 1041-4347. https://doi.org/10.1109/TKDE.2007.250585

[Gia12] Piero Giacomelli. *Hornetq messaging developer's guide* Ed. by Ankita Shashi. Packt Publishing Ltd., 2012.

[Gib01] Phillip B. Gibbons. "Distinct Sampling for Highly-Accurate Answers to Distinct Values Queries and Event Reports". In: *Proceedings of the 27th International Conference on Very Large Data Bases* VLDB '01. San Francisco, CA, USA: Morgan Kaufmann Publishers Inc., 2001, pp. 541–550. ISBN: 1-55860-804-4. URL: http://dl.acm.org/citation.cfm?id=645927.672351

[GK01] Michael Greenwald and Sanjeev Khanna. "Space-efficient Online Computation of Quantile Summaries". In: *Proceedings of the 2001 ACM SIGMOD International Conference on Management of Data*. SIGMOD'01. Santa Barbara, California, USA: ACM, 2001, pp. 58–66. ISBN: 1-58113-332-4. URL: https://doi.org/10.1145/375663.375670. http://doi.acm.org/10.1145/375663.375670.

[GKS01a] Johannes Gehrke, Flip Korn, and Divesh Srivastava. "On Computing Correlated Aggregates over Continual Data Streams". In: *Proceedings of the 2001 ACM SIGMOD International Conference on Management of Data* SIGMOD '01. Santa Barbara, California, USA: ACM, 2001, pp. 13–24. ISBN: 1-58113-332-4. URL: https://doi.org/10.1145/375663.375665. http://doi.acm.org/10.1145/375663.375665

[GKS01b] Sudipto Guha, Nick Koudas, and Kyuseok Shim. "Data-streams and Histograms". In: *Proceedings of the Thirty-third Annual ACM Symposium on Theory of Computing* STOC '01. Hersonissos, Greece: ACM, 2001, pp. 471–475. ISBN: 1-58113-349-9. URL: https://doi.org/10.1145/380752.380841. http://doi.acm.org/10.1145/380752.380841.

[GM98] Phillip B. Gibbons and Yossi Matias. "New Sampling-based Summary Statistics for Improving Approximate Query Answers". In: *SIGMOD Rec.* 27.2 (June 1998), pp. 331–342. ISSN: 0163-5808. URL: https://doi.org/10.1145/276305.276334. http://doi.acm.org/10.1145/276305.276334.

[Gol06] Lukasz Golab. "Sliding Window Query Processing over Data Streams". PhD thesis. University of Waterloo, Aug. 2006.

[GZ10] Lukasz Golab and M. Tamer Zsu. *Data Stream Management*. Morgan & Claypool Publishers, 2010. ISBN: 1608452727, 9781608452729.

[Jai+08] Namit Jain et al. "Towards a Streaming SQL Standard". In: *Proc. VLDB Endow* 1.2 (Aug. 2008), pp. 1379–1390. ISSN: 2150-8097. URL: https://doi.org/10.14778/14541591454179. http://dxdoiorg/10.14778/1454159.1454179

[Joh+05] Theodore Johnson et al. "A Heartbeat Mechanism and Its Application in Gigascope". In: *Proceedings of the 31st International Conference on Very Large Data Bases*. VLDB '05. Trondheim, Norway: VLDB Endowment, 2005, pp. 1079–1088. ISBN: 1-59593-154-6. URL: http://dl.acm.org/citation.cfm?id=1083592.1083716

[Kal+08] Robert Kallman et al. "H-store: A High-performance, Distributed Main Memory Transaction Processing System". In: *Proc. VLDB Endow* 1.2 (Aug. 2008), pp. 1496–1499. ISSN: 2150-8097. URL: https://doi.org/10.14778/1454159.1454211. http://dxdoiorg/10.14778/1454159.1454211.

[KKM13] Konstantinos Karanasos, Asterios Katsifodimos, and Ioana Manolescu. "Delta: Scalable Data Dissemination Under Capacity Constraints". In: *Proc. VLDB Endow* 7.4 (Dec. 2013), pp. 217–228. ISSN: 2150-8097. URL: https://doi.org/10.14778/2732240.2732241. http://dxdoi.org/10.14778/2732240.2732241

[Kle02] Jon Kleinberg. "Bursty and Hierarchical Structure in Streams". In: *Proceedings of the Eighth ACM SIGKDD International Conference on Knowledge Discovery and Data Mining* KDD '02. Edmonton, Alberta, Canada: ACM, 2002, pp. 91–101. ISBN: 1-58113-567-X. URL: https://doi.org/10.1145/775047.775061. http://doi.acm.org/10.1145/775047.775061.

[KNR11] Jay Kreps, Neha Narkhede, and Jun Rao. "Kafka: a Distributed Messaging System for Log Processing". In: *NetDB'11* 2011.

[Kre14c] Jay Kreps. "Why local state is a fundamental primitive in stream proc- essing". In: *O'Reilly Media* (July 2014). Accessed: 2017-11-30. URL: https://wwworeillycom/ideas/why-local-state-is-a-fundamental-primitive-in-stream-processing.

[KW17] Kostas Kloudas and Chris Ward. "Complex Event Processing with Flink: An Update on the State of Flink CEP". In: *data Artisans Blog* (Nov. 2017). Accessed: 2017-12-26. URL: https://dataartisans.com/blog/complex-event-processing-flink-cep-update.

[Lam+12] Valerie Lampkin et al. *Building smarter planet solutions with MQTT and IBM WebSphere MQ Telemetry*. IBM Redbooks, 2012.

[Li+05] Jin Li et al. "Semantics and Evaluation Techniques for Window Aggregates in Data Streams". In: *Proceedings of the 2005 ACM SIGMOD International Conference on Management of Data* SIGMOD '05. Baltimore, Maryland: ACM, 2005, pp. 311–322. ISBN: 1-59593-060-4. URL: https://doi.org/10.1145/1066157.1066193. http://doi.acm.org/10.1145/1066157.1066193.

[Lin+04] X. Lin et al. "Continuously maintaining quantile summaries of the most recent N elements over a data stream". In: *Proceedings. 20th International Conference on Data Engineering*. 2004, pp. 362–373. https://doi.org/10.1109/ICDE.2004.1320011.

[Lin+05] Xuemin Lin et al. "Stabbing the sky: efficient skyline computation over sliding windows". In: *21st International Conference on Data Engineering (ICDE'05)* 2005, pp. 502–513. https://doi.org/10.1109/ICDE.2005.137.

[Ma+05] Lisha Ma et al. "Stream Operators for Querying Data Streams". In: *Advances in Web-Age Information Management: 6th International Conference, WAIM 2005, Hangzhou, China, October 11–13, 2005. Proceedings*. Ed. by Wenfei Fan, Zhaohui Wu, and Jun Yang. Berlin, Heidelberg: Springer Berlin Heidelberg, 2005, pp. 404–415. ISBN: 978-3-540-32087-6. URL: https://doi.org/10.1007/11563952_36. https://doi.org/10.1007/11563952_36.

[MAEA05a] Ahmed Metwally, Divyakant Agrawal, and Amr El Abbadi. "Duplicate Detection in Click Streams". In: *Proceedings of the 14th Interna- tional Conference on World Wide Web*. WWW '05. Chiba, Japan: ACM, 2005, pp. 12–21. ISBN: 1-59593-046-9. URL: https://doi.org/10.1145/1060745.1060753. http://doi.acm.org/10.1145/1060745.1060753.

[MAEA05b] Ahmed Metwally, Divyakant Agrawal, and Amr El Abbadi. "Efficient Computation of Frequent and Top-k Elements in Data Streams". In: *Proceedings of the 10th International Conference on Database Theory*. ICDT '05. Edinburgh, UK: Springer-Verlag, 2005, pp. 398–412. ISBN: 3-540-24288-0, 978-3-540-24288-8. URL: https://doi.org/10.1007/9783540-30570-5_27. http://dxdoiorg/10.1007/978-3-540-30570-5_27.

[MBP06]   Kyriakos Mouratidis, Spiridon Bakiras, and Dimitris Papadias. "Continuous Moni-
          toring of Top-k Queries over Sliding Windows". In: *Proceedings of the 2006 ACM
          SIGMOD International Conference on Management of Data* SIGMOD '06. Chicago,
          IL, USA: ACM, 2006, pp. 635–646. ISBN: 1-59593-434-0. URL: https://doi.org/10.
          1145/1142473.1142544. http://doi.acm.org/10.1145/1142473.1142544.
[MM02]   Gurmeet Singh Manku and Rajeev Motwani. "Approximate Frequency Counts over
          Data Streams". In: *Proceedings of the 28th International Conference on Very Large
          Data Bases* VLDB '02. Hong Kong, China: VLDB Endowment, 2002, pp. 346–357.
          URL: http://dl.acm.org/citation.cfm?id=1287369.1287400.
[Mot+03] Rajeev Motwani et al. "Query Processing, Approximation, and Resource Management
          in a Data Stream Management System". In: *CIDR*. 2003.
[Nar17]   Neha Narkhede. "Exactly-once Semantics are Possible: Heres How Kafka Does it".
          In: *Confluent Blog* (June 2017). Accessed: 2017-11-18. URL: https://www.confluent.
          io/blog/exactly-once-semantics-are-possible-heres-how-apache-kafka-does-it/.
[Nat]   *Does NATS guarantee message delivery?* Accessed: 2018-05-28. Cloud Native Com-
          puting Foundation. 2018. URL: https://nats.io/documentation/faq/#gmd.
[Nel17]   Derek Nelson. "PipelineDB 0.9.7 – Delta Streams and Towards a Post- greSQL
          Extension". In: *PipelineDB Blog* (Mar 2017). Accessed: 2017-11-25. URL:
          https://www.pipelinedb.com/blog/pipelinedb-0-9-7-delta-streams-and-towards-a-
          postgresql-extension.
[Pal13]   Mark Palmer. "How To Analyze Sensor Data In Real-Time With CEP". In: *The
          StreamBase Event Processing Blog* (Apr.2013). Accessed: 2018-02-14. URL: http://
          streambase.typepad.com/streambase_stream_process/2013/04/time-windowing.html.
[Pan15]   Gene Pang. "Scalable Transactions for Scalable Distributed Database Systems". PhD
          thesis. EECS Department, University of California, Berkeley, 2015. URL: http://
          www2.eecs.berkeley.edu/Pubs/TechRpts/2015/EECS-2015-168.html.
[Pipa]   *Streams*. Accessed: 2017-11-25. PipelineDB. 2017. URL: http://docs.pipelinedb.com/
          streams.html.
[Pipb]   *Two Phase Commits* Accessed: 2016-10-17. PipelineDB. 2015. URL: http://enterprise.
          pipelinedb.com/docs/two-phase.html#two-phase.
[PS06]   Kostas Patroumpas and Timos Sellis. "Window Specification over Data Streams".
          In: *Proceedings of the 2006 International Conference on Current Trends in Data-
          base Technology* EDBT'06. Munich, Germany: Springer-Verlag, 2006, pp. 445–464.
          ISBN: 3-540-46788-2, 978-3-540-46788-5. URL: https://doi.org/10.1007/11896548_
          35. http://dx.doi.org/10.1007/11896548_35.
[PT05]   A. Pavan and Srikanta Tirthapura. "Range-Efficient Computation of F" over Massive
          Data Streams". In: *Proceedings of the 21st International Conference on Data Engi-
          neering* ICDE '05. Washington, DC, USA: IEEE Computer Society 2005, pp. 32–43.
          ISBN: 0-7695-2285-8. URL: https://doi.org/10.1109/ICDE.2005.118. https://doi.org/
          10.1109/ICDE.2005.118
[RRH13]   David Rüdiger, Moritz Roidl, and Michael ten Hompel. "Towards Agile and Flex-
          ible Air Cargo Processes with Localization Based on RFID and Complex Event
          Processing". In: *Dynamics in Logistics: Third International Conference, LDIC 2012
          Bremen, Germany, February/March 2012 Proceedings*. Ed. by Hans-Jörg Kreowski,
          Bernd Scholz-Reiter, and Klaus-Dieter Thoben. Berlin, Heidelberg: Springer Berlin
          Heidelberg, 2013, pp. 235–246. ISBN: 978-3-642-35966-8. URL: https://doi.org/10.
          1007/978-3-642-35966-8_19. https://doi.org/10.1007/978-3-642-35966-8_19.
[Ryv+06] E. Ryvkina et al. "Revision Processing in a Stream Processing Engine: A High-Level
          Design". In: *22nd International Conference on Data En- gineering (ICDE'06)* 2006,
          pp. 141–141. https://doi.org/10.1109/ICDE.2006.130.
[San18]   Salvatore Sanfilippo. *Redis*. Accessed: 2018-05-10. 2018. URL: https://redis.io/.

[SCZ05]   Michael Stonebraker, Uğur Cetintemel, and Stan Zdonik. "The 8 Requirements of Real-time Stream Processing". In: *SIGMOD Rec.* 34.4 (Dec. 2005), pp. 42–47. ISSN: 0163–5808. URL: https://doi.org/10.1145/1107499.1107504. http://doi.acm.org/10.1145/1107499.1107504.

[SH12]   S. Senthamilarasu and M. Hemalatha. "Load shedding techniques based on windows in data stream systems". In: *2012 International Conference on Emerging Trends in Science, Engineering and Technology (INCOSET)*. 2012, pp. 68–73. https://doi.org/10.1109/INCOSET.2012.6513883.

[SW04]   Utkarsh Srivastava and Jennifer Widom. "Flexible Time Management in Data Stream Systems". In: *Proceedings of the Twenty-third ACM SIGMOD-SIGACT-SIGART Symposium on Principles of Database Systems*. PODS '04. Paris, France: ACM, 2004, pp. 263–274. ISBN: 158113858X. URL: https://doi.org/10.1145/1055558.1055596. http://doi.acm.org/10.1145/1055558.1055596.

[Tat+03] Nesime Tatbul et al. "Load Shedding in a Data Stream Manager". In: *Proceedings of the 29th International Conference on Very Large Data Bases - Volume 29*. VLDB '03. Berlin, Germany: VLDB Endowment, 2003, pp. 309–320. ISBN: 0-12-722442-4. URL: http://dl.acm.org/citation.cfm?id=1315451.1315479.

[Ter+92] Douglas Terry et al. "Continuous Queries over Append-only Databases". In: *SIGMOD Rec.* 21.2 (June 1992), pp. 321–330. ISSN: 0163–5808. https://doi.org/10.1145/141484.130333. URL: http://doi.acm.org/10.1145/141484.130333.

[TP06]   Yufei Tao and Dimitris Papadias. "Maintaining sliding window skylines on data streams". In: *IEEE Transactions on Knowledge and Data Engineering* 18.3 (2006), pp. 377–391. ISSN: 1041–4347. https://doi.org/10.1109/TKDE.2006.48.

[Tre15]   Tyler Treat. "You Cannot Have Exactly-Once Delivery". In: *Brave New Geek* (Mar. 2015). Accessed: 2018-07-22. URL: https://bravenewgeek.com/you-cannot-have-exactly-once-delivery/.

[Tre17]   Tyler Treat. "You Cannot Have Exactly-Once Delivery Redux". In: *Brave New Geek* (June 2017). Accessed: 2018-07-22. URL: https://bravenewgeek.com/you-cannot-have-exactly-once-delivery-redux/.

[Tuc+03] P. A. Tucker et al. "Exploiting punctuation semantics in continuous data streams". In: *IEEE Transactions on Knowledge and Data Engineering* 15.3 (2003), pp. 555–568. ISSN: 1041–4347. https://doi.org/10.1109/TKDE.2003.1198390.

[Vin16]   Paul Vincent. "CEP Tooling Market Survey 2016". In: *complexevents.com* (May 2016). Accessed: 2017-12-14. URL: http://www.complexevents.com/2016/05/12/cep-tooling-market-survey-2016/.

[VRR10]   Kreimir Vidakovi, Thomas Renner, and Sascha Rex. *Marktübersicht Real-Time Monitoring Software: Event Processing Tools im Überblick*. Tech. rep. Fraunhofer Verlag, Fraunhofer-Informationszentrum Raum und Bau IRB, 2010.

[Wid05]   Jennifer Widom. "The Stanford Data Stream Management System". In: *Microsoft Research Lectures* (July 2005). lecture video (relevant part: 25m45s to 26m48s); Accessed: 2018-07-30. URL: https://www.microsoft.com/en-us/research/video/the-stanford-data-stream-management-system/.

[Apa18a] Apache Software Foundation. *ActiveMQ*. Accessed: 2018-05-10. 2018. URL: https://activemq.apache.org/.

[Apa18f] Apache Software Foundation. *Qpid*. Accessed: 2018-05-10. 2018. URL: https://qpid.apache.org/.

[IBM14]   IBM Corporation. *Of Streams and Storms*. Tech. rep. IBM Software Group, 2014.

[Piv18]   Pivotal Software, Inc. *RabbitMQ*. Accessed: 2018-05-10. 2018. URL: https://www.rabbitmq.com/.

[Çet+16] Uğur Çetintemel et al. "The Aurora and Borealis Stream Processing Engines". In: *Data Stream Management*: Processing *High-Speed Data Streams*. Ed. by Minos Garofalakis, Johannes Gehrke, and Rajeev Rastogi. Berlin, Heidelberg: Springer Berlin Heidelberg, 2016, pp. 337–359. ISBN: 978-3-540-28608-0.

Chapter 5
General-Purpose Stream Processing

Unlike data stream management systems that are mostly intended for analyzing structured information through declarative query languages, systems for stream processing expose generic and imperative (i.e. non-declarative) programming interfaces to work with structured, semi-structured, and entirely unstructured data. Rather than yet another approach for querying data, stream processing can thus be seen as the latency-oriented counterpart to batch processing. In this chapter, we provide an overview over some of the most popular distributed stream processing systems currently available and highlight similarities, differences, and trade-offs taken in their respective designs.

5.1 Architectural Patterns

In contrast to traditional data analytics systems that collect and periodically process huge—static—volumes of data, streaming analytics systems avoid putting data at rest and process it as it becomes available, thus minimizing the time a single data item spends in the processing pipeline. Stream processing pipelines often routinely achieve end-to-end latencies of several seconds or even subsecond latency.

Figure 5.1 illustrates typical layers of a streaming analytics pipeline. Data like user clicks, billing information, or unstructured content such as images or text messages are collected from various places inside an organisation and then moved to the streaming layer (e.g. a queuing system like Kafka [KNR11] or Kinesis [Ama18]) from which it is accessible to a stream processor that performs a certain task to produce an output. This output is then forwarded to the serving layer which might for example be an analytics web GUI like trending topics at Twitter or a database where a materialized view is maintained.

In an attempt to combine the best of both worlds, an architectural pattern called the **Lambda Architecture** [MW15] has become quite popular that complements

© The Author(s), under exclusive license to Springer Nature Switzerland AG 2019   57
W. Wingerath et al., *Real-Time & Stream Data Management*, SpringerBriefs in
Computer Science, https://doi.org/10.1007/978-3-030-10555-6_5

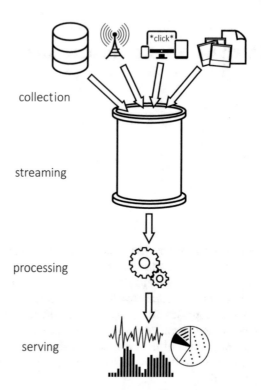

Fig. 5.1   An abstract view on a streaming analytics pipeline

the slow batch-oriented processing with an additional real-time component and thus targets both the *Volume* and the *Velocity* challenge of Big Data [Lan01] at the same time. As illustrated in Fig. 5.2a, the Lambda Architecture describes a system comprising three layers: Data is stored in a *persistence layer* like HDFS [Shv+10] from which it is ingested and processed by the *batch layer* periodically (e.g. once a day), while the *speed layer* handles the portion of the data that has not yet been processed by the batch layer, and the serving layer consolidates both by merging the output of the batch and the speed layer. The obvious benefit of having a real-time system compensate for the high latency of batch processing is paid for by increased complexity in development, deployment, and maintenance. If the batch layer is implemented with a system that supports both batch and stream processing (e.g. Spark), the speed layer often can be implemented with minimal overhead by using the corresponding streaming API (e.g. Spark Streaming) to make use of existing business logic and the existing deployment. For Hadoop-based and other systems that do not provide a streaming API, however, the speed layer is only available as a separate system. Using an abstract language like Summingbird [Boy+14] to write the business logic enables automatic compilation of code for both the batch and the stream processing system (e.g. Hadoop and Storm) and thus eases development in those cases where batch and speed layer can use (parts of) the same business logic, but the overhead for deployment and maintenance still remains.

Another approach that, in contrast, dispenses with the batch layer in favor of simplicity is known as the **Kappa Architecture** [Kre14b] and is illustrated in Fig. 5.2b. The basic idea is to not periodically recompute all data in the batch layer, but to do all computation in the stream processing system alone and only perform recomputation when the business logic changes by replaying historical data. To achieve this, the Kappa Architecture employs a powerful stream processor capable

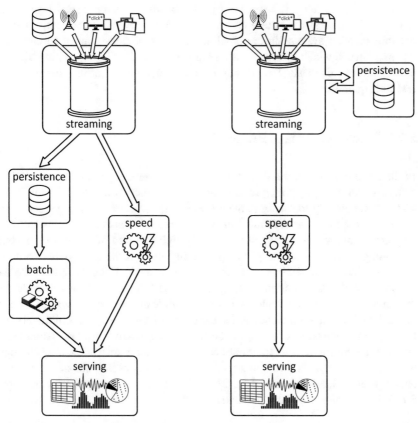

(a) The Lambda Architecture achieves low latency by complementing a batch-oriented with a stream-oriented processing system.

(b) The Kappa Architecture relies on stream-oriented processing only.

Fig. 5.2 Lambda and Kappa Architecture in comparison

of coping with data at a far greater rate than it is incoming and a scalable streaming system for data retention. An example of such a streaming system is Kafka which has been specifically designed to work with the stream processor Samza in this kind of architecture. Archiving data (e.g. in HDFS) is still possible, but not part of the critical path and often not required as Kafka, for instance, supports retention times in the order of weeks. On the downside, however, the effort required to replay the entire history increases linearly with data volume and the naive approach of retaining the entire write stream may have significantly greater storage requirements than periodically processing the new data and updating an existing database, depending on whether and how efficiently the data is compacted in the streaming layer. As a consequence, the Kappa Architecture should only be considered an alternative to the Lambda Architecture in applications that do not require unbounded retention times or allow for efficient compaction (e.g. because it is reasonable to only keep the most recent value for each given key).

Of course, the latency displayed by the stream processor (speed layer) alone is only a fraction of the end-to-end application latency due to the impact of the network or other systems in the pipeline. But it is obviously an important factor and may dictate which system to choose in applications with strict timing SLAs. In the context of this thesis, low latency is particularly important in order to provide real-time queries.

5.2 Batch vs. Stream Processing

While all stream processors share some common ground regarding their underlying concepts and working principle, an important distinction between the individual systems that directly translates to the achievable speed of processing (i.e. latency) is the processing model as illustrated in Fig. 5.3: Handling data items immediately as they arrive minimizes latency at the cost of high per-item overhead (e.g. through messaging), whereas buffering and processing them in batches yields increased efficiency, but obviously increases the time the individual item spends in the data pipeline. Purely stream-oriented systems such as Storm and Samza provide very low latency and relatively high per-item cost, while batch-oriented systems achieve unparalleled resource-efficiency at the expense of latency that is prohibitively high for real-time applications. The space between these two extremes is vast and some systems like Storm Trident and Spark Streaming employ micro-batching strategies to trade latency against throughput: Trident groups tuples into batches to relax the one-at-a-time processing model in favor of increased throughput, whereas Spark Streaming restricts batch size in a native batch processor to reduce latency.

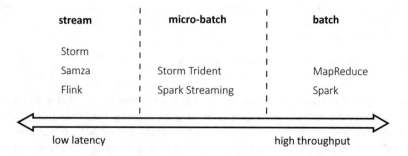

Fig. 5.3 Choosing a processing model means trading off latency against throughput

5.3   State-of-the-Art Stream Processing Frameworks

In the following, we go into more detail on the specificities of the above-mentioned systems and highlight inherent trade-offs and design decisions.

5.3.1   Storm

Storm has been in development since late 2010, was open-sourced in September 2011 by Twitter, and eventually became an Apache top-level project in 2014. It is the first distributed stream processing system to gain traction throughout research and practice and was initially promoted as the "Hadoop of realtime" [Mar12, Mar14], because its programming model provided an abstraction for stream-processing similar to the abstraction that the MapReduce paradigm provides for batch processing. But apart from being the first of its kind, Storm also has a wide userbase due to its compatibility with virtually any language: On top of the Java API, Storm is also Thrift-compatible [SAK07] and comes with adapters for numerous languages such as Perl, Python, and Ruby. Storm can run on top of Mesos [Hin+11], as a dedicated cluster, or even on a single machine. The vital parts of a Storm deployment are a **ZooKeeper** [Hun+10] cluster for reliable coordination, several **supervisors** for execution, and a **Nimbus** server to distribute code across the cluster and take action in case of worker failure; in order to shield against a failing Nimbus server, Storm allows having several hot-standby Nimbus instances. Storm is scalable, fault-tolerant, and even elastic as work may be reassigned at runtime. As of version 1.0.0, Storm provides reliable state implementations that survive and recover from supervisor failure. However, Storm's state management is only feasible for applications with small state, because updates are persisted *synchronously* and therefore can dominate latency when they are large. Earlier versions of Storm only provided the option of stateless processing and thus required state management at the application level to achieve fault tolerance and elasticity in stateful applications. Storm excels at speed and thus is able to perform in the realm of low double-digit milliseconds when carefully tuned (for example, see [Ges+17, Sec. 6.3]). Through the impact of network latency and garbage collection, however, real-world topologies usually do not display consistent end-to-end latency below 50 ms [Gro+15, Ch. 7].

A data pipeline or application in Storm is called a **topology**. As illustrated in Fig. 5.4, a topology is a directed graph that represents data flow as directed edges between nodes which again represent the individual processing steps: The nodes that ingest data and thus initiate the data flow in the topology are called **spouts** and emit **tuples** to the nodes downstream which are called **bolts** and do processing, write data to external storage, and may send tuples further downstream themselves. Storm comes with several **groupings** that control data flow between nodes, e.g. for shuffling or hash-partitioning a stream of tuples by some attribute value, but also allows arbitrary custom groupings. By default, Storm distributes spouts and bolts across the nodes in the cluster in a round-robin fashion, although the scheduler is pluggable to account for scenarios in which a certain processing step has to be executed on a particular node, for example because of hardware dependencies. The application logic is encapsulated in a manual definition of data flow and the spouts and bolts which implement interfaces to define their behaviour during startup, and on data ingestion or on receiving a tuple, respectively.

While Storm does not provide any guarantee on the order in which tuples are processed, it does provide the option of at-least-once processing through an **acknowledgement** feature that tracks the processing status of every single tuple on its way through the topology: Storm will replay a tuple, if any bolt involved in processing it explicitly signals failure or does not acknowledge successful processing

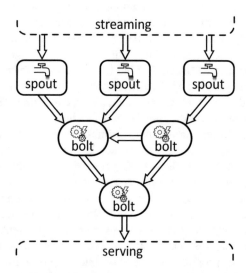

Fig. 5.4 Data flow in a Storm topology: Data is ingested from the streaming layer and then passed between Storm components, until the final output reaches the serving layer

within a given timeframe. Using an appropriate streaming system, it is even possible to shield against spout failures, but the acknowledgement feature is often not used in practice, because the messaging overhead imposed by tracking tuple **lineage** (i.e. a tuple and all the tuples that are emitted on its behalf) noticeably impairs achievable system throughput [Chi+15]. With version 1.0.0, Storm introduced a **backpressure** mechanism to throttle data ingestion as a last resort whenever data is ingested faster than it can be processed. If processing becomes a bottleneck in a topology without such a mechanism, throughput degrades as tuples eventually time-out and are either lost (at-most-once processing) or replayed repeatedly to possibly time-out again (at-least-once processing), thus putting even more load on an already overburdened system.

Storm Trident

Storm Trident was released in autumn 2012 and version 0.8.0 as a high-level API with stronger ordering guarantees and a more abstract programming interface with built-in support for joins, aggregations, grouping, functions, and filters. In contrast to Storm, Trident topologies are **directed** *acyclic* **graphs (DAGs)** as they do not support cycles; this makes them less suitable for implementing iterative algorithms and is also a difference to plain Storm topologies which are often wrongfully described as DAGs [Sto], but actually can introduce cycles. Also, Trident does not work on individual tuples, but on micro-batches. Correspondingly, Trident introduces batch size as a parameter to increase throughput at the cost of latency which, however, may still be as low as several milliseconds for small batches [Eri14]. All batches are by default processed in sequential order, although Trident can also be configured to process multiple batches in parallel. On top of Storm's scalability and elasticity, Trident provides its own API for fault-tolerant state management with exactly-once processing semantics. In more detail, Trident prevents data loss by using Storm's acknowledgement feature and guarantees that every tuple is reflected only once in persistent state by maintaining additional information alongside state and by applying updates transactionally. As of writing, two variants of state management are available: One only stores the sequence number of the last-processed batch together with current state, but may block the entire topology when one or more tuples of a failed batch cannot be replayed (e.g. due to unavailability of the data source), whereas the other can tolerate this kind of failure, but is more heavyweight as it also stores the last-known state. Irrespective of whether batches are processed in parallel or one by one, state updates have to be persisted in strict order to guarantee correct semantics. As a consequence, their size and frequency can become a bottleneck and Trident can therefore only feasibly manage small state.

5.3.2   Samza

Samza [Nog+17, Ram15] is very similar to Storm in that it is a stream processor with a one-at-a-time processing model and at-least-once processing semantics. It was initially created at LinkedIn, submitted to the Apache Incubator in July 2013 and was granted top-level status in 2015. Samza was co-developed with the queuing system **Kafka**[1] [KNR11] and therefore relies on the same messaging semantics: Streams are partitioned and **messages** (i.e. data items) inside the same partition are ordered, whereas there is no order between messages of different partitions.

---

[1]In 2016, a native stream processor was introduced to Kafka: **Kafka Streams** [Kre16] is not only conceptually similar to Samza, but was also built by the same people, reusing portions of the Samza source code [PM16]. Kafka Streams can therefore be considered an unofficial Samza successor.

Even though Samza can work with other queuing systems, Kafka's capabilities are effectively required to use Samza to its full potential and therefore it is assumed to be deployed with Samza in this book. In comparison to Storm, Samza requires a little more work to deploy as it does not only depend on a ZooKeeper cluster, but also runs on top of Hadoop YARN [Apa16h] for fault tolerance: In essence, application logic is implemented as a **job** that is submitted through the Samza YARN client which has YARN then start and supervise one or more **containers**. Scalability is achieved through running a Samza job in several parallel **tasks** each of which consumes a separate Kafka partition; the degree of parallelism, i.e. the number of tasks, cannot be increased dynamically at runtime. Similar to Kafka, Samza focuses on support for JVM-languages, particularly Java. Contrasting Storm and Trident, Samza is designed to handle *large amounts of state* in a fault-tolerant fashion by persisting state in a local database and replicating state updates to Kafka. By default, Samza employs a key-value store for this purpose, but other storage engines with richer querying capabilities can be plugged in.

As illustrated in Fig. 5.5, a Samza job represents one processing step in an analytics pipeline and thus roughly corresponds to a bolt in a Storm topology. In stark contrast to Storm where data is directly sent from one bolt to another, though, output produced by a Samza job is always written back to Kafka from where it can be consumed by other Samza jobs. Although a single Samza job or a single Kafka persistence hop may delay a message by only a few milliseconds [Kre14a], latency adds up and complex analytics pipelines comprising several processing steps eventually display higher end-to-end latency than comparable Storm implementations.

Fig. 5.5 Data flow in a typical Samza analytics pipeline: Samza jobs cannot communicate directly, but have to use a queuing system such as Kafka as message broker

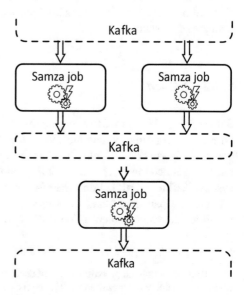

On the upside, however, this design also decouples individual processing steps and thus eases development. Another advantage is that buffering data between processing steps makes (intermediate) results available to unrelated parties, e.g. other teams in the same company. Further, it eliminates the need for a backpressure algorithm, since there is no harm in the backlog of a particular job filling up temporarily, given a reasonably sized Kafka deployment. Since Samza processes messages in order and stores processing results durably after each step, it is able to prevent data loss by periodically checkpointing current progress and reprocessing all data from that point onwards in case of failure; in fact, Samza does not support a weaker guarantee than at-least-once processing, since there would be virtually no performance gain in relaxing this guarantee. While Samza does not provide exactly-once semantics, it allows configuring the checkpointing interval and thus offers some control over the amount of data that may be processed multiple times in an error scenario.

5.3.3   Spark Streaming

Spark [ZCD+12] is a batch processing framework that is often mentioned as the inofficial successor of Hadoop as it offers several benefits in comparison, most notably a more concise API resulting in less verbose application logic and significant performance improvements through in-memory caching. In particular, iterative algorithms (e.g. machine learning algorithms such as k-means clustering or logistic regression) are accelerated by orders of magnitude, because data is not necessarily written to and loaded from disk between every processing step. In addition to these performance benefits, Spark provides a variety of machine learning algorithms out-of-the-box through the **MLlib** library. Originating from UC Berkeley in 2009, Spark was open-sourced in 2010 and was donated to the Apache Software Foundation in 2013 where it became a top-level project in February 2014. It is mostly written in Scala and has Java, Scala, and Python APIs. The core abstraction of Spark are distributed and immutable collections called **RDDs** (resilient distributed datasets)[2] that can only be manipulated through deterministic operations. Spark is resilient to machine failures by keeping track of any RDD's **lineage**, i.e. the sequence of operations that created it, and checkpointing RDDs that are expensive to recompute, e.g. to HDFS [Shv+10]. A Spark deployment consists of a cluster manager for resource management (and supervision), a **driver program** for application scheduling, and several **worker** nodes to execute the application logic. Spark runs on top of Mesos, YARN, or in standalone mode in which case it may be used in combination with ZooKeeper to remove the **master node** (i.e. the cluster manager) as a single point of failure.

---

[2]On top of RDDs, Spark provides DataFrames and Datasets as even more abstract APIs that impose a schema on the otherwise unstructured RDD tuples [Dat18].

Spark Streaming [ZDL+13] shifts Spark's batch processing approach towards real-time requirements by chunking the stream of incoming data items into small batches, transforming them into RDDs, and processing them as usual. It further takes care of data flow and distribution automatically. Spark Streaming has been in development since late 2011 and became part of Spark in February 2013. Being a part of the Spark framework, Spark Streaming had a large developer community and also a huge group of potential users from day one, since both systems share the same API and since Spark Streaming runs on top of a common Spark cluster. Thus, it can be made resilient to failure of any component [Ven+15] like Storm and Samza and further supports dynamically scaling the resources allocated for an application. Data is ingested and transformed into a sequence of RDDs which is called **DStream** (discretized stream) before processing through workers. All RDDs in a DStream are processed in order, whereas data items inside an RDD are processed in parallel without any ordering guarantees. In consequence, the order in which data items are processed may diverge from the order in which they are received, roughly by the batch size. Since there is a certain job scheduling delay when processing an RDD, batch sizes below 50 ms tend to be infeasible [Apa16e, Sec. "Performance Tuning"]. Accordingly, processing an RDD takes around 100 ms in the best case, although Spark Streaming is designed for latency in the order of a few seconds [ZDL+13, Sec. 2]. To prevent data loss even for unreliable data sources, Spark Streaming grants the option of using a **write-ahead log (WAL)** from which data can be replayed after failure. State management is realized through a **state DStream** that can be updated through a DStream transformation.

5.3.4   Flink

Flink [Apa16c] is a project that has many parallels to Spark Streaming as it also originated from research and advertises the unification of batch and stream processing in the same system, providing exactly-once guarantees for the stream programming model and a high-level API comparable to that of Trident. Formerly known as Stratosphere [ABE+14], Flink entered the Apache Incubator under its current name in mid-2014, received top-level status in January 2015 [Apa15], and reached stable version 1.0.0 in March 2016 [Apa16a]. In contrast to Spark Streaming, Flink is a native stream processor and does not rely on batching internally. Apart from the batching API and the streaming API in the focus of this section, Flink also provides APIs for graph processing, complex event processing, SQL, and an executer to run Storm topologies [Sax15]. Flink can be deployed using a resource negotiator such as YARN or Mesos, but also in standalone mode directly on machines. A Flink deployment has at least one **job manager** process (with optional standbys for failover) to coordinate checkpointing and recovery and for receiving Flink **jobs**. The job manager also schedules work across the **task manager** processes which usually reside on separate machines and in turn execute the code. Resource allocation for a job was initially static [Ewe16], but dynamic scaling has been added in version 1.5 in May 2018 [Hue18].

Conceptually, Flink can be considered one of the more advanced stream processors as many of its core features were already considered in the initial design and not just added as an afterthought as opposed to Spark's streaming API or state management in Storm, for instance. However, only relatively few big players have committed to using it in production so far (cf. [Apa16f, Apa16b]). To provide exactly-once processing guarantees, Flink uses an algorithm grounded in the Chandy-Lamport algorithm for distributed snapshots [CL85]: Essentially, **watermark items** are periodically injected into the data stream and trigger any receiving component to create a checkpoint of its local state. On success, the entirety of all local checkpoints for a given watermark comprise a **distributed global system checkpoint**. In a failure scenario, all components are reset to the last valid global checkpoint and data is replayed from the corresponding watermark. Since data items may never overtake watermark items (which are therefore also called *barriers*), acknowledgment does not happen on a per-item basis and is consequently much more lightweight than in Storm. Flink implements a back pressure mechanism [CTE15] through buffers with bounded capacity: Whenever ingestion is overtaking processing speed, the data buffers effectively behave like fixed-size blocking queues and thus slow down the rate at which new data enters the system. By making the buffering time for data items configurable, Flink promotes an explicit trade-off between latency and throughput and can sustain higher throughput than Storm. But while Flink is also able to provide consistent latency below 100 ms, it cannot satisfy as aggressive latency goals as Storm [Chi+15].

Flink provides several APIs to execute *collection-based* (relational) queries: The only distinction between the functionally equivalent **Table and SQL APIs** [HWJ17] is that the first is integrated into the host programming language whereas the latter executes standardized SQL queries as the name implies. The **DataStream API** [Wal17] offers an abstraction to perform complex *stream-based* queries, including operators for windowed aggregations and stream joins. By inserting all tuples within a data stream into an ever-growing and initially empty **dynamic table** [HWJ17], collection-based queries become applicable to streaming data. While *continuous queries* over dynamic tables are push-based and follow collection-based semantics like the self-maintaining queries discussed in Chap. 3, they do not reflect historical data, but only tuples that have arrived since table creation. Therefore, Flink's continuous queries bear similarity to PipelineDB's continuous views (see Chap. 4) rather than real-time queries as provided by real-time databases like Meteor or Baqend (cf. Chap. 3).

5.3.5   *Further Systems*

In the last couple of years, a great number of stream processors have emerged that all aim to provide high availability, fault tolerance, and horizontal scalability. Much like Flink, **Apex** [Apa18b] is a native stream processor that promises high performance in stream and batch processing with low latency in streaming workloads. It has been in development since 2012, was accepted as Apache Incubator project in August 2015 and was granted top-level status in April 2016 [Apa16g]. It is also complemented by a host of database, file system, and other connectors as well as pattern matching, machine learning, and more algorithms through an additional library, called Apex-Malhar. Compared to projects like Spark Streaming or Flink, Apex has only few contributors and little development activity [Apa18e]. **Heron** [Kul+15] was developed to replace Storm at Twitter and is completely API-compatible to Storm, but improves on several aspects such as backpressure, efficiency, resource isolation, multi-tenancy, ease of debugging, and performance monitoring. It was open-sourced in May 2016 [Ram16]. **MillWheel** [ABB+13] is an extremely scalable stream processor that offers similar qualities as Flink and Apex, e.g. state management and exactly-once semantics. Millwheel and FlumeJava [Cha+10] are the execution engines behind Google's **Dataflow** cloud service for data processing. Like other Google services and unlike most other systems discussed in this section, Dataflow is fully managed and thus relieves its users of the burden of deployment and all related troubles. The Dataflow programming model [Aki+15] combines batch and stream processing and is also agnostic of the underlying processing system, thus decoupling business logic from the actual implementation. The runtime-agnostic API was open-sourced in 2015 and has evolved into the Apache **Beam** [Apa18c] project (short for *B*atch and str*eam*) to bundle it with the corresponding execution engines (*runners*): As of writing, Apex, Flink, Spark and the proprietary Google Dataflow cloud service are supported. Another fully managed stream processing system is **IBM Infosphere Streams** [BBF+10]. In contrast to Google Dataflow which is documented to be highly scalable (quota limit for customers: 1000 compute nodes [Data]), it is hard to find evidence for high scalability of IBM Infosphere Streams; performance evaluations made by IBM [IBM14] only indicate it performs well in small deployments with up to a few nodes. **Photon** [Ana+13] is a system developed by Google to join distributed data streams under exactly-once processing semantics. In contrast to the other stream processors discussed here, Photon is designed for geographically distributed deployments. Thus, Photon exhibits relatively high end-to-end latencies in the order of several seconds on average and is specifically designed to cope with infrastructure degradation and failure (such as data center outages) in automatized fashion. **Quill** [Cha+16] is a distributed platform that supports temporal and relational data analysis of historical and streaming data. It uses the analytics library **Trill** [Cha+14] for relational and temporal data analysis. Since Trill relies on micro-batching to compute incremental output over data streams, latency is typically in the order of seconds, even though it is configurable through batch size. **Concord**

[Bro15] is a proprietary stream processing framework designed around performance predictability and ease-of-use. To remove garbage collection as a source of possible delay, it is implemented in C++. To facilitate isolation in multi-tenant deployments, Concord is tightly integrated with the resource negotiator Mesos. Flume [Apa16d] is a system for efficient data aggregation and collection that is often used for data ingestion into Hadoop as it integrates well with HDFS and can handle large volumes of incoming data. While it is not designed for complex topologies, Flume does support simple operations such as filtering or modifying incoming data through **Flume Interceptors** [Gro+15, Ch. 7] which may be chained together to form a low-latency processing pipeline. The list of distributed stream processors goes on, but we consider systems out of scope that have been discontinued (e.g. Muppet [LLP+12], S4 [Neu+10]), or focus on mobile computing (e.g. Sonora [Yan+12]).

5.4 Design Decisions and Trade-Offs

Table 5.1 sums up the properties of those systems in direct comparison which we covered in-depth in the last section. Storm provides low latency, but does not offer ordering guarantees and is often deployed providing no delivery guarantees at all, since the per-tuple acknowledgement required for at-least-once processing effectively doubles messaging overhead. Stateful exactly-once processing is available in Trident through idempotent state updates, but has notable impact on performance and even fault tolerance in some failure scenarios. Samza is another native stream processor that has not been geared towards low latency as much as Storm and puts more focus on providing rich semantics, in particular through a built-in concept of state management. Having been developed for use with Kafka in the Kappa Architecture, Samza and Kafka are tightly integrated and share messaging semantics; thus, Samza can fully exploit the ordering guarantees provided by Kafka. Spark Streaming effectively unifies batch and stream processing and offers a high-level API, exactly-once processing guarantees, and a rich set of libraries, all of which can greatly reduce the complexity of application development. However, being a native batch processor, Spark Streaming loses to its contenders with respect to latency [Chi+15].

5.5 Summary and Discussion

With current technology, it has become feasible to build Big Data analytics pipelines that process data items as they arrive. However, processing latency is involved in a number of *trade-offs* with other desirable properties such as throughput, fault tolerance, reliability (processing guarantees), and ease of development. Throughput can be optimized by buffering data and processing it in batches to reduce the impact of messaging and other overhead per data item, whereas this obviously

Table 5.1 Storm/Trident, Samza, Spark Streaming, and Flink's streaming engine in direct comparison

	Strictest guarantee	Achievable latency	State management	Processing model	Backpressure mechanism	Ordering guarantees	Elastic scalability
Storm	At-least-once	$\ll$100 ms	Yes	One-at-a-time	Yes	No	Yes
Trident	Exactly-once	<100 ms	Yes (small state)	Micro-batch	Yes	Between batches	Yes
Samza	At-least-once	<100 ms	Yes	One-at-a-time	Not required	Within stream partitions	No
Spark Streaming	Exactly-once	<1 s	Yes	Micro-batch	Yes	Between batches	Yes
Flink (streaming)	Exactly-once	<100 ms	Yes	One-at-a-time	Yes	Within stream partitions	Yes

increases the in-flight time of individual data items. Abstract interfaces hide system complexity and ease the process of application development, but sometimes also limit the possibilities of performance tuning. Similarly, rich processing guarantees and fault tolerance for stateful operations increase reliability and make it easier to reason about semantics, but require the system to do additional work, e.g. acknowledgements and state replication. Exactly-once semantics are particularly desirable and can be implemented through combining at-least-once guarantees with either transactional or idempotent state updates, but they cannot be achieved for actions with side effects such as sending a notification to an administrator.

References

[ABB+13] Tyler Akidau, Alex Balikov, Kaya Bekiroglu, et al. "MillWheel: Fault-Tolerant Stream Processing at Internet Scale". In: *Very Large Data Bases*. 2013, pp. 734–746.

[ABE+14] Alexander Alexandrov, Rico Bergmann, Stephan Ewen, et al. "The Strato-sphere Platform for Big Data Analytics". In: *The VLDB Journal* (2014). ISSN: 1066-8888. URL: https://doi.org/10.1007/s00778-014-0357-y. http://dx.doi.org/10.1007/s00778-014-0357-y.

[Aki+15] Tyler Akidau et al. "The Dataflow Model: A Practical Approach to Balancing Correctness, Latency and Cost in Massive-Scale, Unbounded, Out-of-Order Data Processing". In: *Proceedings of the VLDB Endowment* 8 (2015), pp. 1792–1803.

[Ana+13] Rajagopal Ananthanarayanan et al. "Photon: Fault-tolerant and Scalable Joining of Continuous Data Streams". In: *SIGMOD '13* 2013. URL: http://dl.acm.org/citation.cfm?doid$=$2463676.2465272

[BBF+10] Alain Biem, Eric Bouillet, Hanhua Feng, et al. "IBM Infosphere Streams for Scalable, Real-time, Intelligent Transportation Services". In: *Proceedings of the 2010 ACM SIGMOD International Conference on Management of Data*. Indianapolis, Indiana, USA, 2010. ISBN: 978-1-4503-0032-2. URL: https://doi.org/10.1145/1807167.1807291. http://doi.acm.org/10.1145/1807167.1807291.

[Boy+14] Oscar Boykin et al. "Summingbird: A Framework for Integrating Batch and Online MapReduce Computations". In: *Proc. VLDB Endow* 7.13 (Aug. 2014), pp. 1441–1451. ISSN: 2150-8097. URL: https://doi.org/10.14778/2733004.2733016. http://dxdoiorg/10.14778/2733004.2733016.

[Bro15] Cole Brown. "Introducing Concord". In: *Concord Blog* (2015). Accessed: 2016-09-21. URL: http://concord.io/posts/introducing_concord.

[Cha+10] Craig Chambers et al. "FlumeJava: Easy, Efficient Data-Parallel Pipelines". In: *ACM SIGPLAN Conference on Programming Language Design and Implementation (PLDI)*. 2 Penn Plaza, Suite 701 New York, NY 10121-0701, 2010, pp. 363–375. URL: http://dl.acm.org/citation.cfm?id$=$1806638.

[Cha+14] Badrish Chandramouli et al. "Trill: A High-performance Incremental Query Processor for Diverse Analytics". In: *Proc. VLDB Endow*. 8.4 (Dec. 2014),pp. 401–412. ISSN: 2150-8097. URL: https://doi.org/10.14778/2735496.2735503. http://dxdoiorg/10.14778/2735496.2735503.

[Cha+16] Badrish Chandramouli et al. "Quill: Efficient, Transferable, and Rich Analytics at Scale". In: *International Conference on Very Large Databases (PVLDB Vol. 9, Issue. 14)*. 2016. URL: https://www.microsoftcom/enus/research/publication/quill-efficient-transferable-rich-analytics-scale/.

[Chi+15] Sanket Chintapalli et al. "Benchmarking Streaming Computation Engines at Yahoo!" In: *Yahoo! Engineering Blog* (2015). Accessed: 2016-10-17. URL: http://yahooeng.tumblr.com/post/135321837876/benchmarking-streaming-computation-engines-at.

[CL85]   K. Mani Chandy and Leslie Lamport. "Distributed Snapshots: Determining Global
          States of Distributed Systems". In: *ACM Trans. Comput. Syst.* 3.1 (Feb. 1985), pp. 63–
          75. ISSN: 0734-2071. URL: https://doi.org/10.1145/214451.214456. http://doi.acm.
          org/10.1145/214451.214456.
[CTE15]   Ufuk Celebi, Kostas Tzoumas, and Stephan Ewen. "How Apache Flink™ handles
          backpressure". In: *data Artisans Blog* (Aug. 2015). Accessed: 2017-09-12. URL:
          http://data-artisans.com/how-flink-handles-backpressure/.
[Data]   *Google Cloud Dataflow: Resource Quotas.* Accessed: 2016-10-17. Google. 2016.
          URL: https://cloud.google.com/dataflow/quotas.
[Eri14]   Ericsson. "Trident – benchmarking performance". In: *Ericsson Research Blog*
          (2014). Accessed: 2016-01-12. URL: http://www.ericsson.com/research-blog/data-
          knowledge/trident-benchmarking-performance/.
[Ewe16]   Stephan Ewen. "FLIP-6 - Flink Deployment and Process Model - Standalone,
          Yarn, Mesos, Kubernetes, etc." In: *Flink Improvement Proposals* (Aug. 2016).
          Accessed: 2017-11-17. URL: https://cwiki.apache.org/confluence/pages/viewpage.
          action?pageId=65147077
[Ges+17] Felix Gessert et al. "Quaestor: Query Web Caching for Database-as-a-Service
          Providers". In: *Proceedings of the 43rd International Conference on Very Large Data
          Bases* (2017).
[Gro+15] Mark Grover et al. *Hadoop Application Architectures.* Beijing: O'Reilly, 2015. ISBN:
          978-1-4919-0008-6. URL: http://my.safaribooksonline.com/9781491900086.
[Hin+11] Benjamin Hindman et al. "Mesos: A Platform for Fine-grained Resource Sharing
          in the Data Center". In: *Proceedings of the 8th USENIX Conference on Networked
          Systems Design and Implementation.* NSDI'11. Boston, MA: USENIX Association,
          2011, pp. 295–308. URL: http://dl.acm.org/citation.cfm?id=1972457.1972488.
[Hue18]   Fabian Hueske. "Apache Flink 1.5.0 Release Announcement". In: *Apache Flink Blog*
          (May 2018). Accessed: 2018-08-18. URL: https://flink.apache.org/news/2018/05/25/
          release-1.5.0.html
[Hun+10] Patrick Hunt et al. "ZooKeeper: Wait-free Coordination for Internet-scale Systems".
          In: *Proceedings of the 2010 USENIX Conference on USENIX Annual Technical
          Conference* USENIXATC'10. Boston, MA: USENIX Association, 2010. URL: http://
          dl.acm.org/citation.cfm?id=1855840.1855851.
[HWJ17]   Fabian Hueske, Shaoxuan Wang, and Xiaowei Jiang. "Continuous Queries on
          Dynamic Tables". In: *Flink Blog* (Apr. 2017). Accessed: 2017-10-27. URL: https://
          flink.apache.org/news/2017/4/04/dynamic-tables.html.
[KNR11]   Jay Kreps, Neha Narkhede, and Jun Rao. "Kafka: a Distributed Messaging System for
          Log Processing". In: *NetDB'11.* 2011.
[Kre14a] Jay Kreps. "Benchmarking Apache Kafka: 2 Million Writes Per Second (On Three
          Cheap Machines)". In: *LinkedIn Engineering Blog* (Apr. 2014). Accessed: 2016-
          10-17. URL: https://engineering.linkedin.com/kafka/benchmarking-apache-kafka-2-
          million-writes-second-three-cheap-machines.
[Kre14b] Jay Kreps. "Questioning the Lambda Architecture". In: *O'Reilly Media* (July
          2014). Accessed: 2015-12-17. URL: http://radar.oreilly.com/2014/07/questioning-the-
          lambda-architecture.html.
[Kre16]   Jay Kreps. "Introducing Kafka Streams: Stream Processing Made Simple". In:
          Confluent Blog (2016). Accessed: 2016-09-19. URL: http://www.confluent.io/blog/
          introducing-kafka-streams-stream-processing-made-simple/.
[Kul+15] Sanjeev Kulkarni et al. "Twitter Heron: Stream Processing at Scale". In: *Proceedings
          of the 2015 ACM SIGMOD International Conference on Management of Data.*
          SIGMOD '15. Melbourne, Victoria, Australia: ACM, 2015, pp. 239–250. ISBN:
          978-1-4503-2758-9. URL: https://doi.org/10.1145/2723372.2742788. http://doi.acm.
          org/10.1145/2723372.2742788.
[Lan01]   Douglas Laney. *3D Data Management: Controlling Data Volume, Velocity and
          Variety.* Tech. rep. META Group, 2001. URL: http://blogs.gartner.com/doug-laney/
          files/2012/01/ad949-3D-Data-Management-Controlling-Data-Volume-Velocity-
          and-Variety.pdf.

[LLP+12] Wang Lam, Lu Liu, Sts Prasad, et al. "Muppet: MapReduce-style Processing of Fast Data". In: *VLDB 2012* (2012). ISSN: 2150-8097. URL: https://doi.org/10.14778/2367502.2367520. http://dxdoiorg/10.14778/2367502.2367520.

[Mar12] Nathan Marz. "Preview of Storm: The Hadoop of Realtime Processing". In: *BackType Technology Blog* (May 2012). Accessed: 2015-12-17. URL: http://web.archive.org/web/20120509023348/http://tech.backtype.com/preview-of-storm-the-hadoop-of-realtime-processing.

[Mar14] Nathan Marz. "History of Apache Storm and lessons learned". In: *Thoughts from the Red Planet* (Oct. 2014). Accessed: 2015-12-17. URL: http://nathanmarz.com/blog/history-of-apache-storm-and-lessons-learned.html.

[MW15] Nathan Marz and James Warren. *Big Data: Principles and Best Practices of Scalable Realtime Data Systems.* 1st. Greenwich, CT, USA: Manning Publications Co., 2015. ISBN: 1617290343, 9781617290343.

[Neu+10] Leonardo Neumeyer et al. "S4: Distributed Stream Computing Platform". In: *Proceedings of the 2010 IEEE International Conference on Data Mining Workshops* ICDMW '10. Washington, DC, USA: IEEE Computer Society, 2010, pp. 170–177. ISBN: 978-0-7695-4257-7. URL: https://doi.org/10.1109/ICDMW2010.172. https://doi.org/10.1109/ICDMW.2010.172.

[Nog+17] Shadi A. Noghabi et al. "Samza: Stateful Scalable Stream Processing at LinkedIn". In: *Proc. VLDB Endow.* 10.12 (Aug. 2017), pp. 1634–1645. ISSN: 2150-8097. URL: https://doi.org/10.14778/3137765.3137770. https://doi.org/10.14778/3137765.3137770.

[PM16] Pat Patterson and Ted Malaska. "Ingest & Stream Processing – What Will You Choose?" In: *QCon* (Aug. 2016). Accessed: 2018-05-25. URL: https://www.infoq.com/presentations/ingest-stream-processing.

[Ram15] Navina Ramesh. "Apache Samza, LinkedIn's Framework for Stream Processing". In: *thenewstack.io* (2015). Accessed: 2016-09-21. URL: http://thenewstack.io/apache-samza-linkedins-framework-for-stream-processing/.

[Ram16] Karthik Ramasamy. "Open Sourcing Twitter Heron". In: *Twitter Blog* (May 2016). Accessed: 2017-01-15. URL: https://blog.twitter.com/2016/open-sourcing-twitter-heron.

[SAK07] Mark Slee, Aditya Agarwal, and Marc Kwiatkowski. *Thrift: Scalable Cross-Language Services Implementation.* Tech. rep. Accessed: 2018-08-19. Facebook Inc., Apr. 2007. URL: http://thrift.apache.org/static/files/thrift-20070401.pdf.

[Sax15] Matthias J. Sax. "Storm Compatibility in Apache Flink: How to run existing Storm topologies on Flink". In: *Apache Flink Blog* (Dec. 2015).

[Shv+10] Konstantin Shvachko et al. "The Hadoop Distributed File System". In: *Proceedings of the 2010 IEEE 26th Symposium on Mass Storage Systems and Technologies (MSST)* MSST '10. Washington, DC, USA: IEEE Computer Society 2010, pp. 1–10. ISBN: 978-1-4244-7152-2. URL: https://doi.org/10.1109/MSST.2010.5496972. http://dx.doi.org/10.1109/MSST.2010.5496972.

[Sto] *Guaranteeing Message Processing* Accessed: 2018-08-19. Apache Software Foundation. 2018. URL: http://storm.apache.org/releases/1.2.2/Guaranteeing-message-processing.html.

[Ven+15] Bharat Venkat et al. "Can Spark Streaming survive Chaos Monkey?" In: *Netflix Tech Blog* (2015). Accessed: 2016-01-11. URL: http://techblog.netflix.com/2015/03/can-spark-streaming-survive-chaos-monkey.html.

[Wal17] Timo Walther. "From Streams to Tables and Back Again: An Update on Flink's Table & SQL API". In: *Flink Blog* (Mar. 2017). Accessed: 2017-10-27. URL: https://flink.apache.org/news/2017/03/29/table-sql-api-update.html.

[Yan+12] Fan Yang et al. *Sonora: A Platform for Continuous Mobile-Cloud Computing.* Tech. rep. MSR-TR-2012-34. Microsoft Research, 2012. URL: http://research.microsoft.com/apps/pubs/default.aspx?id=161446.

[ZCD+12] Matei Zaharia, Mosharaf Chowdhury, Tathagata Das, et al. "Resilient Distributed
          Datasets: A Fault-tolerant Abstraction for In-memory Cluster Computing". In:
          *Proceedings of the 9th USENIX Conference on Networked Systems Design and
          Implementation* NSDI'12. San Jose, CA: USENIX Association, 2012, pp. 2–2. URL:
          http://dl.acm.org/citation.cfm?id=2228298.2228301.
[ZDL+13] Matei Zaharia, Tathagata Das, Haoyuan Li, et al. "Discretized Streams: Fault-
          tolerant Streaming Computation at Scale". In: *Proceedings of the Twenty-Fourth ACM
          Symposium on Operating Systems Principles*. SOSP '13. Farminton, Pennsylvania:
          ACM, 2013, pp. 423–438. ISBN: 978-1-4503-2388-8. URL: https://doi.org/10.1145/
          2517349.2522737. http://doi.acm.org/10.1145/2517349.2522737.
 [Ama18] Amazon Kinesis. *Amazon Kinesis*. Accessed: 2018-08-19. 2018. URL: https://aws.
          amazon.com/kinesis/.
  [Apa15] Apache Software Foundation. "The Apache Software Foundation Announces
          Apache® Flink™ as a Top-Level Project". In: *Apache Software Foundation Blog*
          (Jan. 2015). Accessed: 2016-11-25. URL: https://blogsapacheorg/foundation/entry/
          the_apache_software_foundation_announces69.
 [Apa16a] Apache Software Foundation. "Announcing Apache Flink 1.0.0". In: *Apache Flink
          Blog* (Mar. 2016). Accessed: 2017-01-15. URL: https://flink.apache.org/news/2016/
          03/08/release-1.0.0.html.
 [Apa16b] Apache Software Foundation. "Apache Flink: Powered By Flink". In: *Apache Flink
          website* (2016). Accessed: 2016-10-17. URL: https://flink.apache.org/poweredby.html.
 [Apa16c] Apache Software Foundation. *Flink* Accessed: 2016-09-18. 2016. URL: https://flink.
          apache.org/.
 [Apa16d] Apache Software Foundation. *Flume* Accessed: 2016-10-17. 2016. URL: https://flume.
          apache.org/.
 [Apa16e] Apache Software Foundation. "Level of Parallelism in Data Processing".
          In: *Spark Streaming – 2.0.0 Documentation* (2016). Accessed: 2016-09-23.
          URL: https://spark.apache.org/docs/2.0.0/streaming-programming-guide.html#level-
          of-parallelism-in-data-receiving.
 [Apa16f] Apache Software Foundation. "Powered By Spark". In: *Apache Spark Website*
          (2016). Accessed: 2016-10-17. URL: https://cwiki.apache.org/confluence/display/
          SPARK/Powered+By+Spark.
 [Apa16g] Apache Software Foundation. "The Apache Software Foundation Announces
          Apache®Apex™ as a Top-Level Project". In: *Apache Software Foundation Blog*
          (Apr. 2016). Accessed: 2016-11-25. URL: https://blogs.apache.org/foundation/entry/
          the_apache_software_foundation_announces90.
 [Apa16h] Apache Software Foundation. *YARN*. Accessed: 2016-10-17. 2016. URL: http://
          hadoop.apache.org/docs/stable/hadoop-yarn/hadoop-yarn-site/YARN.html.
 [Apa18b] Apache Software Foundation. *Apex*. Accessed: 2018-08-18. 2018. URL: http://apex.
          apache.org/.
 [Apa18c] Apache Software Foundation. *Beam*. Accessed: 2018-05-10. 2018. URL: https://beam.
          apache.org/.
 [Apa18e] Apache Software Foundation. *GitHub: Apache Apex Core*. Accessed: 2018-08-18.
          2018. URL: https://github.com/apache/apex-core.
  [Dat18] Databricks Inc. "Resilient Distributed Dataset (RDD)". In: *Databricks Glossary*
          (2018). Accessed: 2018-07-22. URL: https://databricks.com/glossary/what-is-rdd.
 [IBM14] IBM Corporation. *Of Streams and Storms*. Tech. rep. IBM Software Group, 2014.

Chapter 6
State of the Art and Future Directions

The ability to notify clients of changes to their critical data has become an important feature for both data storage systems and application development frameworks. In the final chapter of this book, we summarize the state of the art in push-based data access and identify possible next steps in the development of applications and technology in the field of real-time data management.

6.1 The Big Picture

Table 6.1 sums up the current landscape of systems that provide push-based data access in one form or another.

Traditional (SQL) **database management systems** provide a wealth of features for applications based on request-response interaction, but maintaining query results on a per-user basis is not what they have been designed for. Few SQL systems provide active features beyond triggers and existing functionality for query result maintenance is almost exclusively employed for optimizing pull-based query performance (e.g. materialized views or change notifications). Systems for **Data stream management and processing** are push-based, expressive, and scalable at the same time, but do not provide collection-based query semantics; instead, they rely on the notion of data streams as the basic primitive.

Real-time databases combine the data model of traditional databases with the access model of stream-oriented systems: They follow the same collection-based querying semantics as common databases, but they respond with a continuous stream of informational updates in addition to the initial query result. Even though real-time joins and aggregations are currently not available in any commercial real-time database, their query languages and data models are often comparable (and in some cases virtually identical) to those of typical NoSQL databases: Document stores and real-time databases both focus on sorted filter queries over

© The Author(s), under exclusive license to Springer Nature Switzerland AG 2019
W. Wingerath et al., *Real-Time & Stream Data Management*, SpringerBriefs in
Computer Science, https://doi.org/10.1007/978-3-030-10555-6_6

Table 6.1 An overview over system classes providing push-based data access

	Database management	Real-time databases	Data stream management	Stream processing
Primitive	Persistent collections		Ephemeral streams	
Processing	One-time	One-time + continuous	Continuous	
Access	Random	Random + sequential	Sequential (single-pass)	
Data	Structured			Structured, unstructured

single collections and represent one-to-many relationships through nesting rather than foreign keys. With early real-time databases, developers found themselves evaluating complex performance trade-offs when building reactive applications. However, this is no longer the case for modern systems, because they are able to combine high scalability with query expressiveness on par with MongoDB's. Seeing the immense popularity of NoSQL data modeling today, we are convinced that push-based query features and therefore real-time databases will be gaining traction in the future.

6.2   Real-Time Databases: A New Paradigm for Data Management

We firmly believe that the emergence of scalable real-time databases enables numerous ways to improve existing applications and create genuinely new ones. As a final note in this book, we present three possible ways to innovate application development through scalable systems for real-time data management:

1. **Reactive and Collaborative Mobile Apps.** By providing a push-based access mode for queries, real-time databases ease the development of reactive social media websites, collaborative worksheets, and other applications that promote interaction between users. Since real-time databases provide proactive change notifications for collection-based queries, they specifically appeal to developers that are not experienced or comfortable with the stream-based semantics of DSMSs or stream processing engines.
2. **Upgrading Pull-Based Legacy Interfaces.** Applications that have been developed on top of pull-based databases often work in a pull-based fashion themselves, i.e. the user has to take action to refresh or update her view of the data. However, rather than a deliberate design decision, the need to refresh manually is mostly a mere side effect of using a pull-based database for data storage. Since real-time databases deliver proactive change notifications while following traditional database semantics, we think they could turn existing static interfaces

into self-maintaining ones: Those portions of the user interface that display dynamic information (e.g. user-defined search results) could thus be mended to provide updates proactively as they become available.

3. **Augmenting Current Cache Coherence Schemes.** Even though traditional (relational) database systems are built around a notion of strong consistency, many approaches current schemes for view maintenance and query caching deliberately expose stale data to clients in favor of increased performance: Due to the significant overhead associated with eager incremental query maintenance, in particular, result caches are commonly lagging behind, because they are refreshed asynchronously through batch updates or periodic recomputation. State-of-the-art real-time databases, in contrast, do not have to make this trade-off, since they are designed for low-latency change detection at scale: Instead of pushing result updates to end users, they can simply purge cached query results when they become stale. Thus, real-time databases are natively apt for cache coherence schemes evolving around dynamic data (cf. Quaestor architecture [Ges+17]).

6.3 Closing Thoughts

In the past, practitioners have been rightfully cautious in adopting real-time features for their tech stacks, because they were hard to integrate into existing applications and mostly intractable to use at scale. However, current development in data management technology addresses these issues and thus sparks new confidence in the practicality of easy-to-use systems for push-based data access. With the availability of fault-tolerant stream processing frameworks and scalable real-time databases, even complex access patterns can be expressed and further be served in pull-based and push-based fashion alike. In conclusion to this book, we are confident that real-time data processing and push-based result delivery are finally becoming mainstream features in data management technology.

Reference

[Ges+17] Felix Gessert et al. "Quaestor: Query Web Caching for Database-as-a-Service Providers". In: *Proceedings of the 43rd International Conference on Very Large Data Bases* (2017).